T0333957

A VERY SHORT,
FAIRLY INTERESTING AND
REASONABLY CHEAP BOOK ABOUT

EMPLOYMENT
RELATIONS

FOURTH EDITION

A VERY SHORT,
FAIRLY INTERESTING AND
REASONABLY CHEAP BOOK ABOUT
STUDYING
ORGANIZATIONS

CHRIS GREY

A VERY SHORT,
FAIRLY INTERESTING AND
REASONABLY CHEAP BOOK ABOUT
HUMAN RESOURCE
MANAGEMENT

IRENA GRUGULIS

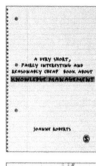

A VERY SHORT,
0 FAIRLY INTERESTING AND
REASONABLY CHEAP BOOK ABOUT
KNOWLEDGE MANAGEMENT

JOANNE ROBERTS

Second Edition

A VERY SHORT,
FAIRLY INTERESTING AND
REASONABLY CHEAP BOOK ABOUT
MANAGEMENT

ANN L. CUNLIFFE

A VERY SHORT,
FAIRLY INTERESTING AND
REASONABLY CHEAP BOOK ABOUT
MANAGEMENT RESEARCH

EMMA BELL AND RICHARD THORPE

A VERY SHORT,
FAIRLY INTERESTING AND
REASONABLY CHEAP BOOK ABOUT
QUALITATIVE RESEARCH

SECOND EDITION

DAVID SILVERMAN

A VERY SHORT,
FAIRLY INTERESTING AND
REASONABLY CHEAP BOOK ABOUT
COACHING AND MENTORING

BOB GARVEY

Second Edition

A VERY SHORT,
FAIRLY INTERESTING AND
REASONABLY CHEAP BOOK ABOUT
STUDYING LEADERSHIP

BRAD JACKSON AND KEN PARRY

A VERY SHORT,
FAIRLY INTERESTING AND
REASONABLY CHEAP BOOK ABOUT
STUDYING CRIMINOLOGY

RONNIE LIPPENS

A VERY SHORT,
FAIRLY INTERESTING AND
REASONABLY CHEAP BOOK ABOUT
INTERNATIONAL BUSINESS

GEORGE CAIRNS AND MARTYNA ŚLIWA

A VERY SHORT,
FAIRLY INTERESTING AND
REASONABLY CHEAP BOOK ABOUT
STUDYING STRATEGY

CHRIS CARTER, STEWART R. CLEGG
AND MARTIN KORNBERGER

A VERY SHORT,
FAIRLY INTERESTING AND
REASONABLY CHEAP BOOK ABOUT
STUDYING MARKETING

JIM BLYTHE

A VERY SHORT, FAIRLY INTERESTING AND REASONABLY CHEAP BOOK ABOUT

EMPLOYMENT RELATIONS

TONY DUNDON, NIALL CULLINANE AND ADRIAN WILKINSON

Los Angeles | London | New Delhi
Singapore | Washington DC | Melbourne

Los Angeles | London | New Delhi
Singapore | Washington DC | Melbourne

SAGE Publications Ltd
1 Oliver's Yard
55 City Road
London EC1Y 1SP

SAGE Publications Inc.
2455 Teller Road
Thousand Oaks, California 91320

SAGE Publications India Pvt Ltd
B 1/I 1 Mohan Cooperative Industrial Area
Mathura Road
New Delhi 110 044

SAGE Publications Asia-Pacific Pte Ltd
3 Church Street
#10-04 Samsung Hub
Singapore 049483

Editor: Delia Martinez-Alfonso
Assistant editor: Lyndsay Aitken
Production editor: Sarah Cooke
Copyeditor: William Baginsky
Proofreader: Tom Hickman
Indexer: Silvia Benvenuto
Marketing manager: Alison Borg
Cover design: Wendy Scott
Typeset by: C&M Digitals (P) Ltd, Chennai, India
Printed in the UK

The title for the 'Very Short, Fairly Interesting and
Reasonably Cheap Book about...' Series was
devised by Chris Grey. His book, *A Very Short, Fairly
Interesting and Reasonably Cheap Book about
Studying Organizations*, was the founding title of this
series.

Chris Grey asserts his right to be recognized as
founding editor of the 'Very Short, Fairly Interesting
and Reasonably Cheap Book about...' Series.

Library of Congress Control Number: 2016949399

British Library Cataloguing in Publication data

A catalogue record for this book is available from
the British Library

ISBN 978-1-44629-410-9
ISBN 978-1-44629-411-6 (pbk)

Mum, Dad and Thomas – *Tony*
Jackie, Mam, Dad and Rex – *Niall*
Erin and Aidan – *Adrian*

Contents

About the Authors

Tony Dundon is Professor of Human Resource Management and Employment Relations at Alliance Manchester Business School, The University of Manchester, UK. He is a Fellow of the Academy of Social Sciences (FAcSS), former Chief Examiner for the Chartered Institute of Personnel and Development (CIPD) and former Editor-in-Chief of the *Human Resource Management Journal*.

Niall Cullinane is Senior Lecturer at Queen's University Management School, Queen's University Belfast. He has published previously in *Economic and Industrial Democracy*, *Work Employment and Society*, *Industrial Law Journal* and *Human Relations*.

Adrian Wilkinson is Professor and Director of the Centre for Work, Organisation and Wellbeing at Griffith University, Brisbane, Australia. Prior to his 2006 appointment, Adrian worked at Loughborough University and prior to that Manchester School of Management at the University of Manchester Institute of Science and Technology, UK. Adrian is a Fellow of the British Academy of Management and Academician Fellow of the Academy of Social Sciences and a Fellow of the Australian Academy of Social Sciences. Adrian is Joint Editor-in-Chief of the *Human Resource Management Journal* (HRMJ).

Acknowledgements

There are numerous people we would like to thank who have provided support and helpful comments in the drafting and writing of this book. Lyndsay Aitkin at Sage has been extremely helpful and patient with our delays and revisions. Numerous colleagues provided valuable comments and insights on various drafts on different chapters, particularly pointing out that our jokes can be pretty bad at the best of times. We thank especially: Michael Barry, Tony Dobbins, Martin Fahy, Damian Grimshaw, Brian Harney, Eugene Hickland, Colm McLaughlin, Stephen Mustchin and Peter Prowse.

Introducing
Employment Relations

Buckingham Palace employs summer staff on 'zero-hours' contract

The Independent, 31 July 2015

Amazon's brutal work culture will stay: bottom lines matter more than people

The Guardian, 22 August 2015

Public sector bosses demand huge pay rises: Unions want increases of tens of thousands of pounds to compensate for new taxes on their pensions

Daily Mail, 5 February 2016

Anger could explode on North Sea oil rigs after workers vote for strikes

Socialist Worker, 27 October 2015

Artificial intelligence and robots threaten to unleash mass unemployment, scientists warn

Financial Times, 14 February, 2016

Gender discrimination still rife in British workplaces

The Telegraph, 4 March, 2014

introduction

We open this book with the above headlines not necessarily for their sensational or especially newsworthy quality, but because they capture how central employment relations (ER) are to our contemporary experiences of life. If you make even the most limited of efforts to keep abreast of current affairs, it is pretty difficult to avoid ER issues like the above being presented in the press and wider media. Beyond the fact that such headlines touch on and report very real and prominent issues, like public–private sector divides, bad employment practice, gender discrimination, workplace strife and automation, they also signal a series of deeper issues concerning ideology, power and interests and the way this can shape much of the presentation and the study of ER. All this matters because it raises questions as to what and who ER is for. It matters also because ER shapes so much of our lives. Joanna Biggs has captured this very well in her book *All Day Long: A Portrait of Britain* (2015), wherein she documents the varied experiences as well as trials and tribulations of a multitude of people doing all sorts of jobs: shoe makers, lawyers, cleaners, crofter, a giggle-doctor, barista, among many others in their places of work. And the experience of employment is indeed highly variable: in *Life Interrupted* (2015), Denise Brennan has recounted the world of employment as experienced by many migrant workers who are trafficked into forced labour in the United States. One of her opening stories is of a young Mexican, Francisco, who jumps from his employer's parked van while at a gas station in California to run directly to police officers he had spotted and to give himself up as an undocumented worker: getting arrested and even deported was a better outcome than remaining in an employment relationship of chattel slavery.

Ultimately, whether you are an attendant for the Queen, a North Sea Oil worker, a civil servant or a manufacturing worker threatened by robots replacing your job in the future, you are most likely in an employment relationship. Or if you're a student, with the aspiration of entering the world of work, then it is most likely that you will very soon be in an employment relationship. An employment relationship, in legal terms, is captured by an employment contract or a contract of service, wherein an employee works for someone else. This is not necessarily as straightforward as it might first sound: the British Court of Appeal established that vicars cannot claim unfair dismissal even if their Church sacks them without good cause. Apparently they work for 'God'.[1] Even the seemingly 'obvious' assumption that someone with an employment contract will get paid for the work they do in exchange for their labour is not necessarily to be taken for granted in these times. In the period between December 2015 and February 2016 there have been approximately 1,000 strikes in China, of which 90 per cent were about 'chronic wage arrears'.[2] In Britain, employment tribunal complaints for 2015 show that 28,000 claims were made for 'unauthorised deductions from wages' and a further 31,000 claims made for 'unpaid holidays'.[3] At the time of writing, security guards who worked hard to help make the 2012 British Olympics such a global success are still waiting for their wages.[4]

For most of us, working under an employment contract is (or will be) the dominant feature of our lives, assuming we are fortunate to avoid the scourge of unemployment or we do not opt out to become self-sufficient sheep farmers in the Scottish Shetland Islands or Australian outback. Ultimately, from the time you leave full-time education to the time you retire, your employment relationship, and your experience of it, will structure most of your waking life. Indeed, even this designation may be inaccurate as those whom we often consider to be outside the labour market, say students and pensioners, are increasingly active in it. Most students, under the pressure of fees, already double-up as workers whilst some retirees have had to return to the labour force to supplement their low pensions in old age.

Yet it is not just that a significant bulk of your life will be spent in employment, it will also affect your wider 'life chances'. Your employment will determine how much you earn, whether you shop in Waitrose or Aldi, or whether your kids will wear counterfeit Adidas or genuine branded Jack Wills. Your employment relationship will determine whether weekends are free for leisure pursuits or spent 'on-call', nervously waiting by the phone in case your manager rings with instructions to attend work. Your employment relations will determine whether working long hours in your job goes by unnoticed, because you love what you do or whether most of your life is spent counting down to a shift's end; like Jimmy Cooper, the post-room boy who lives for the weekends in the film *Quadrophenia*, whose frustration with his job eventually culminates with an explosive rant at his employer and on-the-spot resignation. Employment relations matters also from the point of view of employers, who need to have the 'right' kind of labour at the 'right' time to remain competitive. In the circles of human resource management (HRM), a reasonably cognate area of concern for much ER scholarship, the employee as a 'resource' is often seen as potentially the firm's 'greatest asset'. ER also matters for society as arising from the dynamics of employment relationships at work is the subsequent production and distribution of social wealth and income in our society. It is no exaggeration to say that what happens in employment influences everything from the prices you pay in the shops, the level of unemployment in your community, social class advantage and disadvantage to the outcome of political elections. Many of these issues are not isolated events but are the combined product of various contextual forces that intersect with employment relationships at different times and in different ways: the globalisation of economic conditions, workforce demographics, changing government (state) policies, and growing employer power. So while the tribunal claims we referred to above show an increase in people complaining that their employers have reneged on agreed wages, it is also worth being mindful of the fact that the UK government have decided to make it more difficult (and more costly) for individual workers to pursue such complaints through the various reforms it has made of the system in recent times. Or it might be worth noting that the relative historic rise in individual tribunal claims may be to some extent a by-product of an employment context punctuated by declining trade union representation in contemporary workplaces (Pollert, 2005).

employment relations as a field of study

Let us leave aside these broader issues for the moment and tell you something about the field of ER before we proceed further. It is perhaps fair to say that ER is not strictly a 'discipline' like sociology, economics or psychology which tend to have their own self-contained and established intellectual anchoring points or (in some disciplines at least) widely agreed methodological procedures for acquiring knowledge. In fact sociologists, economists and psychologists have, using their own disciplinary tools and procedures, helped with the study and contributed to our understanding of work and employment. Sociologists might examine what work means to us and to our wider lives, and how employment or occupational identity embeds us in a society; economists might look at transaction costs and incentives or how labour markets are structured; and psychologists often examine how happy or unhappy we are with our work situations. ER is also a hospitable home for historians who might look at how employment has changed over time or provide labour histories; for lawyers the meaning and implications of the contract and legal rights are important; for political scientists examining the notion of work citizenship and governance regimes are key, and even for geographers who consider how physical space is intimately bound up with issues like mobility and regional variation in work and employment (see for example Herod et al., 2007). This broad, interdisciplinary focus means that it is very tempting to characterise ER as a field whose concern is with work and employment, pure and simple.

On the other hand, as one leading commentator has argued, defining ER as broadly about the experiences of work is not entirely satisfactory, because there are some distinct emphases in an ER approach which give it a specific purchase in explaining the world of employment (Edwards, 2003: 4). First, ER scholars tend to focus, as we've said, on situations where an employee works under the authority of an employer and receives a wage in return for his or her labour.

We emphasise *tend to* here, because this is not always strictly true. ER scholars are often concerned with those who are bogusly 'self-employed' or 'on the fringe' of the formal labour market, a strategy sometimes used by less than scrupulous employers to avoid the rights and costs associated with hiring workers legitimately. Also the ER focus *tends to* be distinct from the legal contract of employment as the judiciary might reason. The purely legal conception of employment has been criticised by ER scholars for assuming the contract is made and agreed between equal parties, of equal bargaining strength, and in a market with perfect information. This 'legal figment', as even one of the labour law's leading luminaries observed, conceals a reality of power, submission and inequality (Kahn-Freund, 1972: 8), an idea we'll revert back to at various points in the book. Foregoing the assumption that an agreed contract of employment implies all is subsequently fine and dandy in the relationship, ER scholars point to an ongoing 'indeterminacy' in the exchange that represents the potential for conflictual and cooperative relations. Theoretically, a refined conceptualisation of this relation is 'structural antagonism', first developed by Paul Edwards (1986). The basic idea here is that employers and workers are locked into a relationship of dependency that is compounded by contradictory tensions. These structural tensions can, however, be socially organised by the actors in different ways. Whilst this might seem like a mouthful, it essentially means that employers and workers pull in opposite directions: employers have an interest in making profit and ensuring workers exercise productive effort, whilst workers have an interest in securing high wages and tolerable conditions of work. These tensions, however, do not automatically manifest themselves as conflict, for employers in trying to curtail workers' wages and control their effort have to be mindful to secure worker commitment, whilst workers can equally define and realise their multiple and contradictory interests in numerous ways. Yet whilst workers might, under certain conditions, have an interest in actively cooperating with their employer to ensure the survival of the firm and the continuation of their employment, this does not hide the fundamental point that they remain locked into an antagonistic relationship. We'll see this concept at work later in the book, notably in Chapter 4.

An additional element of an ER focus is on what are often seen as the two parts of the employment relationship, 'market relations' and 'managerial relations'. Market relations relate to the price of labour, in terms of wages or salaries, but also hours of work, holidays and pension rights. Managerial relations on the other hand refer to the relationships that characterise how the consequences of market relations unfold and occur. So the market relations might be one way to set a price for say a certain number of hours of work, but it is also the managerial relations that attempt to settle on how much work is performed in that time, in what ways, and if any sanctions are deployed should workers fail to meet managerial (or agreed) standards. ER is concerned with how the relationship is governed, by whom, and how rules are made that influence working outcomes such as pay, productivity, hours, training, work organisation and so on (Sisson, 2010). Both the market and managerial aspects invite consideration of issues around authority, power and control as well as conflict and cooperation, and raise questions like who makes the rules and how acceptable they are to all parties. Finally, as a field of study, ER is sometimes presented in a systemic fashion that incorporates a particular 'context' of work, which can be shaped by the roles occupied by different employment relations 'actors' and 'institutions' (like employers and workers to name the most obvious ones) who interact through a whole set of 'processes' characterised by conflict and cooperation, themselves premised on a structurally antagonistic relationship. From this flow 'outcomes' such as pay, hours of work, productivity or observation of various laws and regulations. This systemic view of contexts, actors, processes and outcomes also influences the structure of our book.

the focus of this book

Our book is different from the standard instructional texts in the field. Many of these texts, while comprehensive, present something of a detailed description of national laws, arbitration services, employee participation channels, pay arrangements or union structures. This is undoubtedly necessary and desirable. However, while we will discuss institutions, which are important to the subject both in understanding and changing it, our focus is not to explain either British, Australian or US employment systems as such, but to embed issues within a more general discursive interrogation of prominent ER themes for readers who are being introduced to the subject for the first time. Our approach is embedded within the tradition of the *Very Short, Fairly Interesting and Reasonably Cheap* series first inspired by Grey (2005). The book is short so it is not intended to be comprehensive. Rather, as authors we engage in a conversation with you, the reader, about issues and topics in a different way to most textbooks in the area. The conversation is less about how to explain certain rules or give a prescriptive account of the particular merits of a procedure or ER rule per se.

It is written in a way to discuss and reflect on some core ideas central to the field and in a way that, we hope, has a broader appeal for introducing people to the study of ER for the first time. So when we discuss the actors in employment relations, we avoid a description of the evolution and objectives of say employer associations in Britain or Sweden, or the internal structure and organisation of trade unions, and focus instead on the nature of the social relations that characterise the exchanges between employers, managers, workers, unions and the state for example. When we discuss conflict, we focus less on say recounting incidences of strike statistics and the reasons for their decline and instead focus on controversial, political assumptions around the legitimacy of strike action. Our discussion of context focuses less on a standard descriptive and evaluative account of the various discrete factors that are likely to affect different work settings – say the law, technology, product and labour markets – and instead we offer a narrative highlighting the ways in which major contemporary economic and political challenges are a product of, and an influence on, ER developments.

In this regard, we do not intend the book as a substitute for many of the excellent introductory instructional texts in the field, but as a complement. Many of the issues we discuss would possibly make for interesting debate and discussion in classes, seminars, or tutorials alongside the more standard introductory lectures on the components of the ER field. Indeed from our teaching of the subject this often seems to make ER more interesting for students. Learning about how the technical operation of say a mediation hearing or collective bargaining meeting might function in a specific jurisdiction, although important, may lead to description rather than inquisitive and reflective learning around the dynamics of the wider employment experience. Furthermore, in considering issues like authority, power, conflict, cooperation and the like we have been motivated by our experiences of teaching the subject over the years to undergraduate and postgraduate students, typically on a module as part of a wider business, economics, management or law degree. While we have and continue to learn a lot from our students, we have also found that, much like *every* taxi driver we have ever met, they invariably have an opinion on the subject. That everyone has an opinion is inevitable for, as noted above, we nearly all have some experience of an employment relationship. Indeed this is what makes the teaching and learning of the subject enjoyable. On the other hand, opinions are not always well informed and reflect a collection of assumptions, clichés and prejudices of those who have not had the opportunity to properly reflect on the subject. Such viewpoints stem from a mixture of idiosyncratic experience, too many *Daily Mail* or *The Sun* editorials perhaps, or indeed might be the product of a business school education where 'human resource management' – often a student's only other exposure to the area of employment – treats employees as subservient to corporate strategies. 'Cossetted public sector workers', 'striking unions are holding the country to ransom' and 'good communication on management's part can smooth the strains in any employment relationship' are often among the miscellany of ideas or notions about the subject that pervade students' thinking.

It is not that such notions are wrong and many may well be right, but our interest is more about trying to unpack some of these assumptions and reflect on them through a dialogue and conversation with you, the reader. We don't offer any hard and fast answers nor will our book provide you with the right answer to revise for an exam question (but it will probably inform how you might write an answer). Certainly we do hope our conversation through this text might help prompt you to think about everyday ER matters in a different and more critical way. Such critical engagement should help you with your studies, as opposed to the rote learning found on many a business school module involving the repeating of accountancy formulas, four corporate strategy forces, or six or seven pros and cons of a marketing plan (and so on).

an outline of the book

We focus on a selection of key areas of broad interest and debate. Chapter 2 provides a short history of the field before discussing 'different perspectives' about studying employment relations. Chapter 3 considers the wider 'contexts' for employment relations. In this we consider globalisation and how it has evolved to affect, in one way or another, most people's employment condition. We also discuss how some of the big issues that occur today, financialisation, economic crises and austerity, might influence and fit with the study of ER. Chapter 4 is then about different 'actors' who make ER rules about things such as pay, hours of work or voice. It also considers, importantly, why relations between the groups of actors can be complicated and fraught. Then in Chapters 5 and 6 we look at central ER 'processes': Chapter 5 examines the nature of workplace cooperation, while in Chapter 6 we discuss conflict and what happens when workers strike. Chapter 7 looks at key 'outcomes', and we focus here on employee voice as a phenomenon in itself but also the extent to which workers may have a say over substantive matters like their pay and working time. In Chapter 8 a brief conclusion is offered: in this, we engage with business school education, concerns around inequality and technological changes. We suggest how the study of the employment relationship is dynamic, rich and central to a deep understanding about societal issues and broader economic and labour market changes.

2

A Very Short History on Employment Relations and Its Perspectives

introduction

In our last chapter, we discussed how ER as a field of study can be viewed, at one level, as a broad concern about all aspects of work and employment. On the other hand, the field of ER has also tended to have some fairly distinct nuances to its concerns, namely a focus on the regulation of the employment relationship and an associated appreciation of the context, central actors, workplace processes of conflict and cooperation and the various outcomes central to the unfolding of this dynamic. However, two issues are probably worth mentioning here. First, the concerns of ER have never really been static; they have evolved as wider societal change has occurred, so that the research priorities dominating at one particular period reflect the particular problems that prevail at that time. Second, how those concerns have been prioritised, interpreted and explained has often been shaped by the particular lens of analysis that students of the subject have, either consciously or unconsciously, brought with them. So what is a problem under one perspective might not necessarily be a problem for an alternative view of ER. A strike, for instance, can obviously be a problem for someone keen to ensure workplace order and harmony, like say a manager. But for a politically motivated militant, on the other hand, a strike, far from being problematic, is likely to be celebrated as the awakening of the oppressed proletariat who rise up and challenge the power of managers (see, for example, Darlington and Lyddon, 2001). In this chapter we will reflect on two matters: i) the wider concerns of ER as a field as it has developed through time, and ii) the dominant perspectives that have tended to characterise the interpretive frameworks which frequently curry favour in the subject.

a short history of employment relations as a field of study

The modern employment relationship, characterised as it is by the selling of labour to an employer on the market, has its broad roots in the period of the Industrial Revolution of the 18th and 19th centuries. While people certainly toiled in pre-industrial times, it was the arrival of capitalism and the Industrial Revolution where one found the growing domination of a labour market characterised by the buying and selling of labour in exchange for a wage. Whereas relations were a mixture of bondage and patronage in the pre-industrial period of serfs with its 'Lord of the Manor', the labour market under capitalism was one of a contract, based on notions of free exchange and a cold hard cash nexus. The process of transformation was particularly unpleasant; indeed, upon reviewing the genesis of the labour market, Karl Marx (1992) in *Capital* vividly assessed it to have come 'dripping from head to foot, from every pore, with blood and dirt'. On one side stood the money owner – the employer of men, women and children – who possessed great stocks of machinery, tools and raw material. On the other side stood the worker, with nothing to sell but their sweat and toil and the threat of the workhouse should gainful employment prove elusive.

Affixed to this great upheaval was the emergence of the factory system or, in the less favourable language of William Blake, the 'dark Satanic mills'. Production became concentrated on a larger scale requiring more organised control of the growing influx of workers. This task was none too easy for the first pioneers of labour management, as Sidney Pollard's (1963) scholarship on the period identifies. Owners were learning how to manage a great refractory mass of workers, most of whom were ill at ease with the regimentation, monotony and loss of control that marked work under capitalism. Whereas work had previously been shaped by the natural changes of dawn to dusk, the shifting of the tides or the seasons, the new regime demanded that formal requirements of the employer's factory clock dictate the regularities of employment. Indeed the factory clock began to govern life, which explains the tradition of being given a watch on retiring, as your time was now your own and not purchased or owned by your employer. Factories in these times were not how we might recognise them today. They were chaotic and dangerous. Employment relations created enormous social problems both in and outside the factory, as living conditions were dismal. If you read *North and South* by Elizabeth Gaskell

(1998, first published in 1855) – or watch the BBC TV series based on the book – the grim working (and living) conditions of the time are all too stark. Set in the fictional industrial town of Milton – a thinly disguised industrial Manchester – we see the heroine witness the grim working conditions of her life. The novel features a strike as well as the recruitment of an alternative labour force by the employer to undermine the strike. Such conditions were ripe for challenge. Unions or 'combinations' of workers, political parties of a new working class helped ameliorate the harsher edges of industrial capitalism. So too did sections of enlightened or progressive employers, adopting industrial welfare schemes. If you happen to enjoy a bar of Cadbury's chocolate while sitting at the back of a large lecture, or a bowl of Quaker porridge in the morning, then these are the types of employers who pioneered some of the earliest welfare programmes to support workers, including the building of decent housing for the growing mass of factory employees.[5] By the end of the 19th century, economic growth aided by expanding markets and rising labour productivity in many countries was also beginning to raise living standards, whilst simultaneously reinforcing and intensifying massive inequalities of wealth.

Influenced by changing industrial structures, mechanisation and technology as well the demands of war, employers at the start of the 20th century began experimenting with more systematic ways of managing employment. In the steel mills of Philadelphia, the obsessive-compulsive Fredrick Taylor was coming to grips with time and motion study; the US Army were experimenting with psychometric testing to recruit officers; while Henry Ford was stealing ideas about assembly lines from watching pig disassembly on the bloody floors of the Chicago abattoirs. These were the foundations of 'scientific management' which had the effect of 'deskilling' labour. A series of popular movies and symbolic images have, over time, constantly depicted the degradation of the deskilling of work in this period. Charlie Chaplin's famous film *Modern Times* satirises the factory process as adopted by Henry Ford (and others), with his factory worker going round and round trying to tighten screws in what looks like never-ending repetitive work motions, wherever he went. In this depiction, the pace of work is controlled by management using new technologies to get workers to work harder (and faster).

However, workers are not passive dopes, and for reasons discussed in later chapters, they were never entirely keen on the employers' newest or supposedly 'best practice' policy for controlling their labour effort. Time and again workers displayed mistrust over the new-fangled methods of stop watches and so-called human relations ideas for participation (Brown, 1977). They looked on as the new methods raised productivity and wealth and decided that an equitable share in the ever-increasing economic pie was in order. Increasingly workers concluded that they needed greater protection and security in a laissez-faire economy prone to wild bouts of 'boom and bust'. Indeed some, like the syndicalists – radical unionists across Continental Europe and the United States – wanted to scrap the capitalist employment relationship altogether, replacing it with socialism. Nor were workers content to live under the benevolent despotism of employer paternalism. Outside the factory gates, workers were increasingly taught to regard themselves as citizens, with free choices over government and lifestyle. Yet once inside the factory, employers were demanding that these very same citizens subject themselves to autocratic rule. In sum, workers increasingly wanted more control over the conduct and fruit of their labour. Instincts to challenge the prevailing order grew stronger, encouraging collective organisation amongst workers, first in unions of skilled men but later too the unskilled and women.

Yet like one street gang encroaching upon another's 'turf', employers were none too keen about this intrusion onto 'their patch'. The issue of control over labour effort ensued and became the industrial capitalist equivalent of gang warfare. Indeed, like gangs at war, blood was spilt, although it was usually the owners (using the police and military) who did the spilling. The Welsh Llanelli Riots of 1911, the Dublin Lockout of 1913, the American Ludlow Massacre of 1914, the Swedish Ådalen Shootings in 1931 all testify to how struggle in employment relations could descend into resistance as well as open violence. This 'war' proceeded at slightly different times, in slightly different ways with slightly different outcomes across different industrialised economies. Inevitably 'truces' were called. For example, Swedish employers and workers agreed to cease hostilities at a spa resort in Saltsjöbaden: the subsequent pact of 1938 became the exemplar of the much-admired 'social democratic compromise' of the 20th century (Korpi, 1983). The Americans, on the other hand, worked out a 'New Deal' reflected industrially in the National Labor Relations Act of 1935: an uneasy truce between employers and organised workers which gave trade unions legal rights to recognition. British employers, across diverse sectors of the economy, similarly worked out agreements with workers, whether in engineering, mining or textiles. An increasingly common backdrop to most of these compromises was a changing economic landscape where, particularly in the aftermath of the Second World War, governments adopted a more interventionist role in their respective national economies: deepening welfare systems, nationalising whole sectors of activity, protecting 'national champions' in industry whilst, under the influence of Keynesianism, manipulating levels of economy-wide demand predominately through fiscal policies aimed at promoting a high-growth/full-employment flavour of mixed capitalism. It was in this broad period that ER as a field of study began to take shape.

employment relations perspectives

One way to appreciate the emergence of a scholarly field in ER is to perhaps think more broadly about social scientists who observe phenomena like rivalry amongst football hooligans or street gangs. Often motivating such scholars is a desire to understand the nature of society: its 'disorder' and 'malintegration' amongst different subcultures, whether on the football terraces or the street corner. In this regard, ER scholars were keen to diagnose the maladies of the workplace, prescribing a course of treatment to create 'order'. Those who subjected work and employment issues to scrutiny tended to come from a wide variety of intellectual backgrounds: institutional economists, historians and lawyers were prominent amongst the first cohort (Frege, 2007). They were also, in the main, politically committed to and predominately of a social democratic persuasion. In Britain the first scholars of the subject were Beatrice and Sidney Webb and G.D.H. Cole, all of whom were committed Fabian socialists. In the United States, one of the early specialists was John Commons, a democratic socialist and critic of neo-classical economics, along with Selig Perlman, a labour historian, economist and promoter of 'bread and butter' business unionism as a counterweight to Marxist theories of political unionism. In the years after the Second World War, as workers increasingly took to unions to negotiate with their employers and government intervention in the area of employment rights grew, the field of scholarship burgeoned. A commonality in points of study was an emphasis on understanding the employment-centred institutions that had emerged and were now central to regulating relations between employers and, increasingly, unionised workers.

The common focus of study was at an industry-wide or workplace level, examining how institutional actors of employers, unions and government agencies interacted to negotiate the rules governing the conduct of the employment relationship. There will be more on these actors in Chapter 4. But what it initially meant was a policy focus on collective bargaining between employers (including the public sector) and unions. The focus was hardly surprising. The relationship between collective bargaining and trade unions was an increasingly important public policy concern of the mid-20th century as the inflationary consequences of full employment and strikes were becoming a political issue. In other ways, too, the forward march of collective bargaining, trade unionism and the 'social democratic compromise' of mixed capitalism seemed to be the inevitable future. By the 1960s, academics like John Dunlop in the US or Hugh Clegg and Allan Flanders in the UK, innovators in defining distinct systems of employment relations (or 'industrial relations' as it was then called), were in high demand for their knowledge, regularly contributing to government commissions, state boards, public policy and industry practice (Ackers, 2007). During these times government often relied on a new cadre of academics – sociologists, economists, labour lawyers – who were studying and researching emerging employment issues, workplace behaviours, issues of industrial strife and ideas about industrial democracy and participation. You may get a sense of the dominance and popularity of these scholars and the roles they were fulfilling in shaping policy and practice by examining the photograph in Exhibit Box 2.1 below, taken at the time.

Exhibit Box 2.1   An ER academic is spotted leaving a government commission hearing on incomes, circa 1968.

Credit: Photo by Stan Meagher/Stringer/Getty Images

In philosophical terms, the position of ER scholars at this time could be summarised as follows: employers and employees hold many opposing interests on various aspects of employment. Consequently, employers should not demand, or expect, absolute or automatic deference to their authority, but rather accept that conflict is a legitimate and inevitable feature of work. Conflicting interests between employers and employees should not be suppressed, but reconciled and negotiated to accommodate the differing demands of each party. The philosophy is sceptical of management theories of work and motivation encouraging unilateral employer regulation without appreciating that conflict was not simply an abnormality to be eradicated with the right supervisory style. The acceptance of inevitable clashes at work, and the preference for negotiation, led to recommendations for institutionalising conflict so as to manage it better. This could be achieved through employer recognition of trade unionism and collective bargaining, and the support of the law where necessary. The preference for unions and collective bargaining was seen as necessary to counter the imbalances of power in the relationship between employer and individual worker (an issue we shall discuss in more detail in Chapter 4). Bargaining was not to be conducted with free abandon whatever the consequence. It should rather be conducted within limits that avoided dysfunctional economic and social costs for society. The philosophy of these scholars has tended to be termed 'pluralist' and probably was (and is) the dominant orthodoxy of most ER scholarship.

As the 1970s progressed, the pluralist philosophy of ER seemed much like the contemporary 'progressive-rock' of Pink Floyd and Emerson, Lake and Palmer that sound-tracked the era: an unrivalled force. However, as the decade progressed, pluralism became subject to an intellectual challenge in much the same way as the smooth, placid sounds of 'prog-rock genre' were confronted by the arrival of a noisy, aggressive 'punk rock'. Instead of Iggy Pop and The Sex Pistols, however, the challenge came from Marxist and left-radical scholars (for the sake of simplicity, we'll refer to this philosophy as *radicalism*). Much like Johnny Rotten's sneer, the radical philosophy was a product of its time. By the mid- to late 1970s, the long boom of the post-war decades had come to a halt across many industrialised economies. Unemployment was on the rise, as was inflation, whilst strikes and industrial disputes had become commonplace. In the United States, the media had coined the mood of the time as the 'Lordstown syndrome'. This referenced the General Motors (GM) plant at Lordstown, Ohio, and the 'syndrome' referred to the plant's extraordinary employee absenteeism, turnover and high rates of on-the-job drug and alcohol use, punctuated by walkouts, strikes and sabotage. It was a byword for worker disaffection or alienation that seemed, in some accounts at least, to stalk the industrialised world.

Into this context stepped radical ER scholars who, armed with a crumpled copy of the *Morning Star* in one hand and Harry Braverman's *Labor and Monopoly Capitalism* (1974) in the other, sought to dismantle pluralism. ER, the radicals sneered, should be located in a wider appreciation of capitalism, class struggle and exploitation. Capitalism was built on the exploitative appropriation of the workers' unpaid labour by a capitalist class who held an unjust monopoly over the means of production. This system was illegitimate. The pluralist preference for collective bargaining, the radicals argued, merely sustained a system of gross inequality and privilege. Collective bargaining integrated the working class into the conditions of their own exploitation, while the state, committed to supporting the conditions in which capitalists' social power could be perpetuated, was an active force in sustaining this system of exploitation. Capitalism required not simply social democratic reform, which the radical argued could only be temporary and illusory, but revolutionary transformation towards socialism. Support for worker radicalisation, militancy and resistance ensued.

The arrivals of the radicals onto the scene of employment relations did challenge the pluralist position and, as the photograph below demonstrates (see Exhibit Box 2.2), made for some rather awkward ER conferences and seminars. It produced a series of debates which have, in various ways come to shape how many scholars continue to think about their field (see Heery, 2015). It also brought into play a serious consideration of the role of sociology and heterodox economics for understanding employment relations, and many of the concepts the radicals

Exhibit Box 2.2   A pluralist and coterie of radicals (right) discuss the finer subtleties of the 'balance of power' circa 1982.

Credit: Photo by Steve Eason/Hulton Archive/Getty Images

used in the 1970s have remained important for how we think about the nature of the relationship and will be revisited in this book. Indeed there would be some who would think like radicals, and accept many of their notions about conflict at work, but who may not necessarily agree with the putative links with a wider politicised class struggle in society or the prescription to overthrow capitalism per se (Edwards, 1986).

Whilst the pluralist and radical exchange reflected the changing times of the 1970s, both philosophies were probably unprepared for changes that took hold from the 1980s onwards as post-war systems of national employment relations restructured into something radically different. Much of the orthodox pluralist project of the 1960s, with its mechanisms to control wage inflation and moderate the so-called labour problem of unofficial strikes, generally failed. Subsequent transformation was wrought by the changing nature of capital investment and state policy, often consorting under the label 'globalisation' and discussed more fully in our next chapter. On the one hand, businesses have sought to expand markets and trade to raise profitability, whilst on the other, government – influenced by ideas on market liberalism that increased trade in all financial, business and consumer markets expand wealth and raise living standards – sought to divest from ownership of economic resources and encourage greater competition through privatisation. Assisted by technological and transportation developments as well as international agreements on trade and financial markets brought about by increasingly prominent supranational arrangements like the North American Free Trade Agreement (NAFTA) and the European Union (EU), multinational corporations have exported their capital around the globe in search of the best financial returns. The consequence was often capital flight from traditional, and more expensive, manufacturing heartlands for pastures new, like the unregulated zones of South East Asia. In their wake, a declining manufacturing sector in the developed economies, exposed by foreign competition, has been compensated for by an expanding service sector in finance, insurance, retail, wholesale and hospitality. The employment profile of industrial economies has thereby changed, a feature accentuated by a growing feminisation of labour markets with increasing numbers of female workers – a feature of working life often ignored (Greene, 2003; Wajcman, 2000) – along with expanding migrant participation rates, many in lower paid occupations. Under the pressure of greater competition, firms have been forced to restructure organisations, experimenting with a whole host of new practices like just-in-time systems, quality circles, outsourcing, subcontracting, as well as robotised and automated production. In nearly all industrial economies, the traditional habitat of unions and collective bargaining has receded, particularly in the private sector. Greater competition has encouraged employers to seek or impose new forms of flexibility in the determination of pay, the organisation of working hours and structuring of employment contracts, the latter most notable in the aforementioned rise in part-time and temporary work.

challenging the ER field: rival perspectives of human resource management and neo-liberalism

Allied to the broad developments discussed above and reflecting the changed times have been new philosophies about work and employment. As mentioned in the prior chapter, students today are usually introduced to work and employment through the sponsorship of courses and modules in management, strategy or HRM. Rather than seeing employment as a relationship through a pluralist lens, there is an inherent bias within mainstream managerial writings to treating workers as objects to be subservient to some employer-led strategic mission. Rather than looking at employment as a subject in and of itself, its study, under Strategic HRM, becomes bracketed into a narrow agenda around how skilled managers might be equipped with the latest knowledge of best practice in recruitment, selection, training, development, rewards and performance management. There is little appreciation of institutions and how these matter; rather the insights of American scholars like Jeffrey Pfeffer (1998) and Dave Ulrich (1998) are assumed to have as much validity in Dubai as in Delaware. Some of HRM's reasoning is a re-hash of what ER pluralists once dismissed as 'unitarism'. This refers to a philosophy that assumes that the company will, or should have, a single source of authority, exercised by the employers and accepted by all employees. Conflict, where it exists, is irrational, unnecessary, a product of the wrong policy or misunderstandings amongst the workforce and can be engineered out of an organisation through sophisticated management policy. This vision of work is ambivalent on independent collective bargaining and trade unionism or at best regards them as unnecessary and redundant.

There is little doubt that a flavour of unitarism has managed to portray itself as the modern approach to understanding work, particularly in many mainstream business schools (a point we return to more fully in our final chapter). ER, whether through ideology or ignorance, is often viewed as 'outdated' because of its past associations with unions and collective bargaining. One of the authors, for example, can recall being introduced to a new colleague in his department, a specialist in management strategy. When asked by his new colleague what their specialism was a casual reply of 'employment relations' was met by his new colleague increduously exclaiming, 'I didn't think people research that any more, isn't it called talent management now?' Such sentiments are usually wrapped up in a worldview that thinks contemporary employees are now all white-collar, highly skilled, technologically savvy knowledge workers who are informed of their employment rights and highly discerning of sophisticated strategy or high-performing HRM. This image is, of course, as misguided as the view that all workers prior to the 1980s were a collective behemoth of trade-union-conscious, cloth-capped, donkey-jacketed manual workers who, with kestrels perched on their shoulders, spent their days busing it up and down the country on flying picket duty. The reality is much more complex, subtle and variable and whilst employment *has* dramatically changed, many of the enduring themes of effort, conflict, cooperation and voice, as we will demonstrate in this book, remain as important as ever. Globally, many workplaces are as unpalatable now as they were in the descriptions of the industrial capitalism era that opened this chapter. For much of the global labour force, like say those crammed into factory dormitories in China making our smartphones or the casual workforce comprising the agri-food sector, the faddish corporate nomenclature of 'engagement' and 'talent management' is not only irrelevant but highly ignorant of inequality and employer power.

Consequently ER scholars have looked on the unitarist perspective and a lot of HRM as naive, faddish, illusionary and even positively dangerous in encouraging students of employment to think that it is simply a case of tailoring the right management policy without appreciating the pluralist and radical realities of work. More specifically the response of ER has been twofold: one approach has sought to discriminate between the 'nice words' and 'harsh realities' of unitarist HRM through research into how evidently benign and innovative management policies like 'culture management' or 'teamwork' result in work intensification and exploitation of employees at work. Some of the best work on 'high performance work systems' in recent times has been undertaken by ER academics concerned to assess its impact on employee experiences (Harley et al., 2010; Cushen and Thompson, 2012). A second response has been one of colonisation, where many ER scholars have simply taken up the mantle of teaching and researching HRM in higher education, but from a pluralist or radical perspective (see, for example, Wilkinson et al., 2017). Despite such endeavours there remains general scepticism amongst most ER scholars of the managerial and biased unitarist agenda (Godard, 2014). Indeed the photograph shown below (Exhibit Box 2.3), taken of a chance meeting

Exhibit Box 2.3   Three ER scholars (right) attempt to engage two HRM colleagues (left) in a discussion over the merits of 'talent management', prior to a university faculty meeting. Note how the professionally dressed managerial scholars (left) pretend not to hear their less fashionably dressed ER colleagues.

Credit: Photo by Jimmy Sime/Getty Images

between ER and Strategic HRM departmental colleagues at one university, gives you a sense of the feelings the two camps have for each other.

Whereas HRM has been more open to ER rebuttal and influence, perhaps more threatening to the field of ER is the political and economic philosophy promoting competitive markets and free trade. This neo-liberal philosophy was marginalised in the post-war decades but returned to fashion as developed economies struggled to revive profitability in the crisis of the 1970s. Influenced by a mixture of historians, philosophers of science and economists originally associated with the Mount Perlerin Society, the neo-liberal philosophy would emerge as an influential orthodoxy within policy circles, influencing many of the changes discussed above (Harvey, 2007). Unlike unitarism, however, neo-liberalism recognises that workers do have legitimate and separate interests in the labour market and in the workplace. The problem arises, neo-liberals contend, when workers, in pursuing their interests, undermine or distort the competitiveness of market forces through unionisation and collective bargaining or when the state enacts policies that undermine incentives to work through 'generous' welfare payments. These actions create inefficiencies in how markets allocate scarce resources imposing costs on 'outsiders' like other (non-union) workers, consumers or the productive potential of the wider economy in the form of unemployment, costly goods, inflation or lost wealth (Mankiw, 2015). In effect, the regulatory institutions, beloved of pluralists and at least defended in some form by radicals, impose burdens on employers and restrict competitive markets in ways that are inefficient or 'suboptimal' for society as a whole. As a result, neo-liberals will favour a market rather than institutional allocation to ensure the forces of supply (sellers) and demand (buyers) can oscillate freely and flexibly in response to price signals. Indeed for neo-liberals there are no employment relation problems per se that cannot be addressed through the free play of market forces and unperturbed price signals.

The problem here is that, even at the level of theory, competitive markets produce outcomes that are not always efficient, fair or free (Hahnel, 2015). Theoretically employers, following their own competitive logic, can act inefficiently through using capital-saving, labour-using techniques that are privately profitable but socially inefficient and rejecting capital-using, labour-saving techniques that are socially efficient but privately less profitable. Indeed such behaviour may explain the low productivity malaise in the contemporary UK for example, with its highly liberalised labour market: UK employers have the relative freedom to pursue low investment routes to higher profitability, sweating labour in order to improve profitability rather than upgrading production. Theoretically then, even within the logic of the market, there is scope for what Wolfgang Streeck (1997) terms 'beneficial constraints': regulatory institutions that inhibit short-term market decision making can promote long-term efficiency gains by shutting off low-road, low-skilled cost minimisation in favour of high-road, high-skilled routes.

In practice markets are highly 'imperfect' and rarely kowtow to the perfectly competitive market form. And even in those situations where markets broadly conform to highly competitive scenarios unpalatable 'trade-offs' can ensue. As Thomas Piketty's (2014) highly publicised and rather long work has recently shown, countries moving towards liberalised markets in recent decades tend to be marked by high levels of income inequality which promote a patrimonial capitalism based on inherited wealth. Such inequality, Richard Wilkinson and Kate Pickett argue in their 2009 book *The Spirit Level: Why More Equal Societies Almost Always Do Better*, is strongly associated with a whole host of other socially dysfunctional outcomes like poorer physical and mental health, more drug abuse, more obesity, lower social mobility and lower trust.

Markets, whilst enriching society in some ways, may well polarise it in others. A growing narrative is those at the top of the income ladder do well, those in the middle find themselves squeezed while those at the bottom stagnate or slide into poverty and precariousness (see Sophia Parker's 2013 edited collection, *The Squeezed Middle*). There are of course trade-offs and it would be amiss to ignore evidence suggesting, for example, that flexible labour markets have often tended to outperform their more regulated counterparts in terms of lower levels of unemployment or in readjusting to the disequilibrating forces of recession. But behind the headline figures are significant social and human consequences not always appreciated by those who would uncritically praise liberalised markets but which continue to trouble many ER scholars. The latter would argue that the qualitative experience of employment, the problems of underemployment, the overworked, the de-skilled, bogus self-employment and precarious work are worthy of policy considerations and as equally if not more important than counting the quantity of jobs. In short, job quality is important (Sayer, 2014).

ER perspectives in contemporary terms

For ER scholars, particularly those of a pluralist persuasion, the difference with the neo-liberal perspective is that non-market institutions remain necessary in the employment relationship. Furthermore, ER is distinctive from the unitarist flavour of mainstream HRM, which tends to be managerialist in its focus. For ER there is no slavish adoption of the perspective of the employer without considering the outcomes for workers (and perhaps wider society). A good example of this might be the pluralist position advanced by John Budd (2004). He sees the field of pluralist ER scholarship as focusing on three fundamental objectives of efficiency, equity and voice. Contradicting the economist view of the employment relationship as a purely economic transaction, with business wanting efficiency and workers wanting income, Budd argues that equity and voice are equally important objectives. The traditional narrow focus on efficiency must be balanced with employees' entitlement to fair treatment (equity) and the opportunity to have meaningful input into decisions (voice), he says. Only through greater respect for these human concerns can broadly shared prosperity, respect for human dignity, and equal appreciation for the competing human rights of property and labour be achieved. Budd proposes a fresh set of objectives for modern democracies, 'efficiency, equity, and voice', and supports this triad with an intellectual framework for analysing employment institutions and practices. Extreme positions on any of the three dimensions in the triangle may predict unstable employment relationships. In Budd's view, the aim is to strike a balance between all three: the best of all possible worlds, this perspective would maintain, is the social democratic compromise.

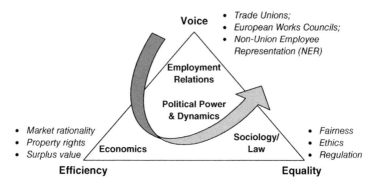

Figure 2.1   Efficiency, equity and voice

Adapted from Budd, 2004

For the ER radicals the response has tended to be different. In its most politicised Marxist form, radicals will argue that rather than save capitalism from itself, which remains as exploitative and unjust as ever, the response to neo-liberal marketisation is resistance and the seeking out of effective modes of struggle whether in the form of new social movements, worker-owned enterprises or a reinvigorated labour movement that can hasten the move to a post-capitalist future (Wolff, 2012). Some radicals have nailed their colours to mobilisation theory and a phoenix from the flames like union revitalisation (Atzeni, 2016). But in many ways, as we noted above, the radical–pluralist divide is probably not as marked as it once was. Differences certainly remain, but the debate has moved on and what remains of both camps is probably now something of a united front against the unitary excesses of human resource management and the untrammelled marketisation favoured by neo-liberalism. Certainly a few purist adherents to their respective variety of pluralism or Marxism still exist (Ackers, 2015; Seifert, 2015), but many scholars continue to go about their business of empirical research without any particularly *conscious* commitment to either camp (which may not necessarily be a good thing!). Most scholars are likely to simply favour, for their underlying theoretical commitments, the concept of the 'structural antagonism' referred to in Chapter 1, a concept which can accommodate pluralist and radical persuasions if need be. This is not to imply that the pluralist–radical debate is now redundant: it is not and still resurfaces with interest and vigour in the pages of many ER academic publications. For example, when the Marxist ER scholars, Martin Upchurch et al. (2009: 8) recently criticised social democratic trade unionism as 'the best possible shell of liberal capitalism', Jelle Visser (2010: 815) responded with pluralist counter:

> If that shell includes the universal welfare state, near full employment, the still relatively high degree of union organisation and participation in workplaces, and the limited degree of inequality found in Scandinavia, most unions would probably settle for it – if only they knew how to get there.

But instead of the field being marked by radicals and pluralists trading blows, the focus of contemporary ER has tended to be preoccupied with the aforementioned structural changes brought about by neo-liberal political economy and globalisation leading to very important research questions like: what are the resilience or otherwise of national institutional arrangements for work and employment in the face of apparently uniform globalised economic pressures? Do institutions of employment relations across countries and sectors increasingly converge to a common type in the face of global market pressures or are national or sectoral institutional arrangements able to absorb these in their own variable and diverging ways? What role do multinational corporations play in this process and how do employment relations practices play out at a transnational level? What are the trends in the determination of pay and organisation of working time and how are divisions over these matters now expressed and organised with the relative decline of union coverage, collective bargaining and strike incidence? Indeed what are the prospects for union and collective bargaining revitalisation? What are the consequences for employment relations in light of 'vertically disintegrated firms' and the rise of global supply chains? How can inequality and disadvantage at work be best addressed? How the answers to these questions are resolved comparatively across both different countries and different sectors are just some of the issues likely to concern contemporary ER perspectives. Institutions have remained central to the analysis with the previous decade in particular marked by a very strong interest in the explanatory possibilities offered by 'varieties of capitalism' (VoC) theory (see Hall and Soskice, 2001; Hancké et al., 2007). Put in a very simple gloss, this perspective says that employers organise, articulate and manage their interests in different ways across different institutional contexts. So German employers face higher levels of strong, centrally organised unionised workers and, in employer associations, bargain with them at industry level. American employers, on the other hand, face less organised and fewer unionised workers, and opt to negotiate wages at the company level. Due to institutional supports for works councils and co-determination rights in workplace participation, German employers often have to cooperate with employees to reach major decisions, while American employers collaborate far less and can usually act as unilateral decision-makers. Studies in this vein have compared work reorganisation in US and German call centres, for example, demonstrating that the German firms adopt high-involvement practices relying on broad skills and worker discretion, while the US firms rely on a narrow division of labour and tight discipline (Doellgast, 2008). The outcomes in this particular study were explained by differences in institutional supports for collective voice: the German works councils used their stronger co-determination rights to encourage alternative, participatory approaches to work design. Yet there is not universal enthusiasm for a brand of explanation that focuses on the detail and distinction of institutionalism across different contexts. One radical scholar of work and employment, Paul Thompson (2010), has criticised much of this analytical endeavour for spending far too much time on the variety and not enough on the capitalism. Similarly, Heyes et al. (2014: 46) argue that instead of an exclusively institutional analysis there is a need to pay attention in ER to the 'concrete relationships between actors within particular capitalist societies...with reference to underlying social relations that are common to capitalist societies'. Even where national variation across ER actors, processes and outcomes occurs, changes in the economic environment, like the contemporary Great Recession, have had a universal result in making employers and the state's attachment to longstanding employment institutions much weaker, creating common pressures for institutional reconstruction in broadly the same direction: towards decentralised, individualised, firm-centred ER institutions offering much greater flexibility and autonomy in the determination of pay and conditions at the firm level (Baccaro and Howell, 2011).

conclusion

This chapter has been a rather ambitious (and short) rundown of the history of ER and the associated intellectual perspectives that emerged out of the field as it developed in the academy. As you can see there is a noticeable diversity in the field which we have tried to pin down through the broad intellectual framings of pluralism and radicalism which often stand apart from the apparent spectres of unitarism and neo-liberalism. Notably we ended with a broad brushstroke account of contemporary ER concerns, noting what we might call the institutional tendency and referencing the influential theory of VoC. We also noted the unease which some scholars have with this preoccupation, suggesting the need for a greater appreciation of the common pressures for liberalisation and the inter-relationships between national ER arrangements and the global economic context of contemporary capitalism. This is a very serviceable point at which to conclude this chapter, for our very next chapter makes an attempt to do that.

3

Casinos, Crises and Cutbacks: The Context for Employment Relations

▰▰▰▰ introduction

Standard fare in mainstream textbooks on ER is often a chapter on 'environment forces'. The idea behind such efforts is to describe the wider contextual influences that shape employment. Typically this amounts to a discrete consideration of technology, politics, law, economics and social trends, and how product and labour markets impact the employment relationship. Accompanying the chapter might even be a few nice charts or one or two reflective questions asking you to consider how technology influences the jobs of people who work in the likes of Burger King or a call centre. But let's be honest, these sorts of chapters can be a little drab, if not also a heavy read. At the risk of some self-deprecation we can say this with some confidence, having been involved in writing such weighty if not also dreary tomes in other not-so-short texts (see Dundon and Rollinson, 2011, Chapter 3; Marchington and Wilkinson, 2012, Chapter 2). Nonetheless, even if some instructional texts which cover environmental forces can be bit of a struggle to get through, an appreciation and conversation about 'context' *is* important in order to engage more fully with issues of state power and employer action, along with worker and union responses. By way of example: imagine you are watching television one evening and haphazardly switch to a channel covering a live football match, a sport we shall suppose you have no interest in. From the information on screen, you can see that the game is 110 minutes in progress and is currently 3-3. As you have no interest in football all this will mean very little to you. You switch channel. Now consider an alternative scenario. You are a keen football fan. Your favourite team is playing, it is a cup final, and despite being regarded as underdogs from the outset, they have come from 3-0 down to push the match into extra time. Penalties beckon. Clearly in this second scenario, the nature of the game, as you observe it, is now completely different. What in the first scenario might amount to little more than an observation of grown men (or women) kicking a polyurethane-covered ball around a pitch would, in the second scenario, have transformed into a heart-thumping, nail-biting clash of epic proportions that you will probably remember for the rest of your days. The circumstances that form the setting for the second scenario then – your love of football, your team in the final, the dramatic comeback – mean that what is otherwise a very simple phenomenon of kicking a ball is now a spectacle of momentous significance.

While we can safely assume that understanding the context of contemporary employment relationships is unlikely to stir the same passions as in our second scenario, appreciating that contexts differ is an important part of studying ER. Describing the actions of employers and employees and their efforts at employment regulation is not nearly enough for appreciating the full magnitude of what is really going on. So in this chapter we will discuss some context of contemporary ER. Rather than evaluate the main contextual factors in discrete self-contained sections, we have decided to take a more discursive overview. We interlink what are impactful social, political, legal and economic influences that shape the subject. Specifically, we reflect on ER in the contemporary context of financialisation, economic crises and the pursuit of austerity. Somewhat impishly we have referred to these in the chapter's title as 'casino' and 'cutback' factors. This is not meant as an evaluative statement per se, but simply to state the obvious: no one really wants to live under conditions of permanent austerity and suffer the disruptions caused by economic crisis, risk and uncertainty that seem to pervade contemporary life resemble an outright gamble.

returning to our very short little bit on history

We continue to live in the long shadow of a global financial crisis, or the Great Recession. For those unschooled in the complexities of financial economics, understanding this recession can be difficult. It can all seem a confusing mix of banks on the precipice, exotic financial instruments and government debt. In many ways, it seems a world apart from the day-to-day stuff of ER, much of which we will discuss in the course of this book. Yet all of the talk of public sector cuts in the news, at least at the time of writing, should give you some inkling that all this stuff matters for ER. In fact it is sometimes not realised that the crisis of today is in fact closely related to long-term, historical trajectories in the employment relationship across advanced economies. Let us explain by wading back through the mists of time.

One of the major obstacles to continued economic growth for employers in the 1970s was labour supply (Armstrong et al. 1991). Scarcities of labour were common across Western Europe and the United States. Workers at this time were frequently well organised, both industrially and politically and, by historical standards, reasonably well paid. Employers, threatened increasingly by a profit squeeze from organised labour, needed access to cheaper and less organised employees. One route to circumvent organised workers was to encourage immigration. So a French employer would seek to import workers from the Maghreb, whilst an English employer might draw on its country's historical ties to former colonies, employing some casual Irish labourers for example. Swedish employers, faced with labour shortages, worked out a deal with Marshal Tito and imported Yugoslavs, whilst German employers often sourced Turkish *Gastarbeiter*.[6] If sourcing migrant labour was not always feasible, another option for employers was new technology. Automating work tasks might be with the aim of raising productivity but, in the process, it could potentially de-skill work and thereby make labour cheaper and easier to control. It also meant workers were substitutable with one another and a firm could shed labour, creating unemployment, which meant managers could more easily discipline those members of organised labour who remained in work (more about this in Chapter 5 on 'Cooperation'). Unsurprisingly, unions would resist such initiatives or at least seek out an appropriate quid pro quo in return: productivity agreements were common, with 'restrictive practices' bought out through bonus payments or wage increases for instance.

Nonetheless, employers at this time could be slow to take up automation. In this post-war period, employers operated in relatively sheltered domestic economies and had less of an incentive to adopt cost-reducing technology. The worlds of trade and commerce were generally less global than they are now. Then, employers could simply pass on increased production costs to their consumers who, in these times of tariffs and quotas, were largely a captured market. There is an important point here about automation adoption, if you will afford us a digression. We return to the issue of new technology and its potential impact on the future of ER in Chapter 8; for now, it is almost impossible to avoid the headline claims, whether from *Financial Times* reports[7] or MIT academics (Brynjolfson and McAfee, 2014), prophesying robots stealing people's jobs in the near future. Despite all current talk about a new automation wave, it is quite likely that employers will not live up to the hype: there may be far too much cheap labour around for employers to risk investment in expensive technologies. Contrary to many of the slogans plastered on the billboards of the typical university business school, many corporations simply do not have some innate potential to 'be innovative' or 'inspire leadership': in fact, many are quite content to live off the fat of the efforts of large pools of cheap and precariously placed workers employed in global supply chains across the world. It also points to an interesting conclusion about technology in the employment relationship. Far from being a neutral force or 'independent variable', the use of technology at work is conditioned by existing hierarchical social relations: namely the balance of power between capital and labour and not some allegedly neutral objective of securing 'efficiency'. You might enjoy, in this regard, David Noble's (2000) historical account of computer numerical control (CNC) machinery, where employers used new technology to dilute craft labour controls over production. It is a matter we will return to in later chapters.

But let's briefly get back to our little bit of recent history. The days of sheltered domestic markets carved up between national champions were eventually undermined by exports from rival industrial nations in the 1980s (most notable here were the Japanese who seem to have per-fected Taylorism in the form of 'lean production'). The response of employers passing on production costs to the consumer was no longer tolerated or seen as legitimate. Aping Japanese production techniques suddenly became the fashion as every employer rushed to adopt some variant of 'total quality management' or 'quality circle'. Pushing through such changes industrially was not always easy although, as recounted in Chapter 2, governments have refashioned a particular environment to help businesses do so. Whether it was Helmut Kohl in Germany, Margaret Thatcher in Britain, or Ronald Reagan in the United States (who had previously eked out an acting career starring in such classics as *Bedtime for Bonzo*, and as former union leader of the Actors Guild of America a key protagonist in the film industry's communist witch-hunt), politicians of a neo-liberal disposition could invariably be relied upon to help boost employers' profitability. This could work in different ways. Combatting the then significant problem of inflation (rising prices) encouraged a curb on the supply of money (through raising interest rates or cutting government spending), which in turn created unemployment and thereby checked wage growth. Politically, new zones of profitability could be prised open by the priva-tisation of national resources and utilities: water, electricity, telecom-munications, transportation, public housing, pensions and health care. But perhaps above all was a new global architecture designed to facili-tate the easy international flow of money to wherever it could be used most profitably (Glyn, 2007). Barriers to trade, such as tariffs and quotas, were reduced and a globally interlinked system of financial markets was constructed through what become known in 1986 as the

'Big Bang', linking London and New York and ultimately the world's major financial markets into one system. Liquid money capital could now scour the globe looking for locations where the return was highest (Harvey, 2011). Global financialisation was born.

In this brave new world the contextual environment had shifted: multinational businesses now had the option to go where the cheapest labour and raw material were on offer, a process facilitated by a radical reorganisation of transport systems like 'containerisation' and developments in information and communication technologies. Whilst multinational corporations and financial assets were now able to roam much more freely, labour, and of course governments, remained rooted in particular nations and localities. The result was competition amongst states keen to maintain or attract investment and jobs through the use of tax breaks. Within multinationals and across their various subsidiary plants, it also encouraged a strategy of 'divide and rule': threatening to move production and jobs elsewhere to where wages and working conditions are cheaper. Writing at the dawn of this period, Keith Cowling (1982: 145) observed:

> [Employers] become increasingly nomadic...It will be privately efficient for each transnational corporation to adopt such a nomadic existence, reflecting as it does an appropriate response to rising labour costs [in the West] and the opportunities offered by a more flexible technology...Wherever workers act to raise wages or control the intensity or duration of work they will lose their jobs to other groups of less well organised and less militant workers in other countries. Thus de-industrialisation is a consequence of class struggle in such a world.

If labour becomes scarce or radicalised, then enter on stage the Mexican *Maquiladoras* and Filipino *Export Processing Zones* to supply cheaper and unorganised workers. Add to the mix the dismantlement of socialism in Eastern Europe and Deng Xiaoping's shift to a state regulated variety of capitalism in China, then access to global labour becomes not only plentiful but cheap (Bellamy-Foster and McChesney, 2012). Another consequence was the feminisation of labour as more women entered into the labour market, often to take up low-paid, insecure work producing in turn highly unequal experiences for many female workers (Rubery and Rafferty, 2013). But if employers thought the labour supply problem was now solved, a glut of employment would create a combination of stagnant and downward pressure on wage growth, particularly for those whose skills were now redundant or among those with no skills at all. Englebert Stockhammer (2012) has observed that one of the hallmarks of this process has been a progressive polarisation of income across Germany, France, Japan and to a lesser extent the US and the UK, as wages as a percentage of output fell significantly from the 1980s onwards. We shall return to the consequences of this later and consider wage inequalities and income distribution in Chapter 8.

financialisation unleashed

Several well-known movies capture the so-called multiplier of economic wealth from financial capitalism: the classic 1987 *Wall Street*, its 2010 remake *Money Never Sleeps* or the 2015 comedy–drama *The Big Short* (among others) all chart, in different ways, the rise and fall of financial capital and the ensuing global financial crisis on businesses and millions of employees. For many major employers and multinational conglomerates the new wave of globalisation was like a swanky party gone wild. Employer concerns about a possible labour shortage problem were solved, new markets prised-open gave access to untapped wealth, workers' bargaining power was considerably weakened and taxation burdens minimised or even removed. While there are winners and losers among businesses and workers, the globalisation era was something of a profit boom for speculators and many multinational employers. The narrative ran that if employers are given incentives to invest and 'create' more wealth, they will have more profit left over to invest in their business, and thereby create more jobs. This, in turn, will feed through into a rise in income for all. At one level the idea sounds logical: if investors at the top of the food chain have more money to invest, the positive multiplier is more spending, economic growth and employment, and in time workers lower down the social and economic ladder will receive higher wages. In a way, 'greed' for lack of a better word, 'is good', as Gordon Gekko, the billionaire investor of Oliver Stone's *Wall Street* claimed. There is a theory for the idea, captured in Exhibit Box 3.1, known as 'trickle down' economics.

At another level the whole idea of 'trickle down' economics can be seen as a cloak for ideological and self-serving rationales for the powerful. Ha-Joon Chang (2014) has pointed out that it frequently seems that to get the rich to work harder we need to make them richer by, say, cutting taxes on their profits; yet to get the poor to work harder, specifically, say, the unemployed, we often have to make them poorer by cutting welfare benefits that are said to act as a disincentive

"Maybe it evaporates before it gets down to us."

Exhibit Box 3.1   Trickle down economic theory.

© CartoonStock (www.CartoonStock.com). Used with permission

to work. Of course, while employers *can* invest their surplus profits into expanding production or job creation activities, they do not necessarily *have* to. Furthermore, while many can and do opt to invest, it is not necessarily in the 'real economy'. Rather, significant bodies of investors have increasingly directed their wealth into asset values and the stock markets, which had the unfortunate effect of encouraging asset bubbles of various sorts, and usually have dysfunctional consequences for the wider economy and society.

Indeed, as Bellamy-Foster and Magdoff (2009) have recounted, the excess profits employers have enjoyed in the period of globalisation have been a key factor in the expansion of so-called 'financialisation', that is, the increasing dominance of financial institutions and credit/debt in the economy. With the glut of excess profits, financial institutions like banks, hedge funds and private equity companies stepped forward with a range of new and complex investment instruments: futures, credit default swops, derivatives were all designed to help the surplus capital find profitable investments. Indeed headline employers and traditional producers like Ford, Porsche, General Electric and General Motors got actively involved in credit markets through setting up mortgage divisions in their corporations. In the years before its infamous bankruptcy, Enron was supposed to be an energy company, but it had increasingly made most of its money trading in the derivatives and futures markets. In 2003 General Motors, one of America's largest employers and iconic car manufacturers earned more than $800 million, not from the making of its cars and trucks, but from investments in mortgages and finance loans. In that same year its car and truck operations earned GM just $83 million (Rubery, 2015). In countries like the United States and Britain, the financial sector, encapsulated in Wall Street investment banks and the City of London, have become the key respective hubs of both economies (often, it must be said, at the expense of their country's manufacturing sectors).

However, it is not unreasonable to suggest that financial institutions theoretically play a serviceable economic role: for example, lending, options, derivatives, etc. can release resources that might otherwise remain idle, providing funding for other economic activity that would not have taken place. But that is only a small fraction of the real story and argument. It is more plausible to appreciate that financial institutions simply allow creditors to profit from other people's productivity, hence the now famous reference to Goldman Sachs as a 'vampire squid' by that eminent source of economic commentary, *Rolling Stone* magazine.[8] Ultimately, financial firms and their employees make nothing, that is, nothing apart from the recirculation of money that has no productive outcome. Sure, a lot of glamour is associated with working in the likes of 'The Gherkin' in London, but often the actual work amounts to little more than someone mouse-clicking buttons on a screen, moving money from those who want to save it to those who want to invest it, profiting on the difference accrued in interest rates. If we imagine Gordon Gekko again, from the *Wall Street* movie, the whole process is seen as 'capitalism at its finest … money itself isn't lost or made, it's simply transferred … I create nothing.' Sayer (2014) eloquently explains that these types of earnings have no contribution to productive value. Interestingly, an understanding of this is clearly expressed by Gekko's opponent in the *Wall Street* film, Carl Fox, the blue collar trade union steward at the airline company Gekko is trying to asset strip, when he remarked that instead of creating something useful, Gekko and his ilk are simply 'living off the buying and selling of others'.

The sort of behaviour the likes of Gekko are advocating, when unregulated, can also generate serious efficiency losses and externalities for the economy. As banks found new ways of accessing funds and new avenues for making profits in the 1990s and 2000s, through the aid of integrated financial markets and global capital movements, they found that instead of waiting for money to be deposited, they could source cheap loans from another financial institution. That is, more casino betting at the blackjack table. Instead of waiting for the maturity on some loan, banks could simply repackage and sell the loan on to another financial institution. This was the fate of the mortgage loans of the 2000s, the result of which was the sharing out of risk across many financial institutions. Financial activity as a proportion of a country's entire economic activity burgeoned in this period. As David Harvey (2011: 29), the radical geographer notes, 'why invest in [relatively] low profit production when you can borrow in Japan at a zero rate of interest and invest in London at 7 per cent whilst hedging your bets on a possible deleterious shift in the yen-sterling exchange rate?'

We will return to some of the major consequences of this behaviour further below, but it is perhaps worth thinking about the impact of financialisation on the day-to-day of employment relations. An anecdote may illustrate. In the mid-2000s, IBM entered into an agreement with stockholders to deliver $10 earnings per share by 2010, a strategy internally known as 'Roadmap 2010'. To achieve its targets, IBM had to find ways to increase profit margins and generate quick cash returns for shareholders. Invariably this led to a short-term focus on cutting costs and seeking out efficiencies in various business operations across the company. The cash generated from such cost-cutting and boosting of margins was then handed over to shareholders in the form of dividends. The strategy to deliver $10 by 2010 proved successful and indeed IBM's share price rose 91 per cent between 2002 and 2010 (notably a later attempt to replicate this strategy, 'Roadmap 2015', failed however with the result that stockholders dumped IBM stock, causing the company's share price to slump). Those executives who delivered on the 2010 Roadmap to the shareholders were duly rewarded; the then CEO, Sam Palmisano, for example, received a package of over $200 million when he exited the company in 2010. Reflecting on his success, Palmisano recounted:

> We gave investors annual outlooks, and we gave them earnings. You have to give them something, they're owners. In 2006 we told Wall Street that we would go from $6 to $10 in earnings per share by 2010. Basically, the shareholders were just asking us to be friendly with capital allocation. They wanted more margin expansion and cash generation than top-line growth, because they knew that if we generated cash, we'd give it back to them in the form of a share buyback or a dividend, not a crazy large acquisition that no one else could see value in. (Denning, 2014[9])

On the contrary, market analysts outside the company claimed IBM was perhaps too 'friendly with capital allocation' and that its pursuit of rising earnings per share was built on wilting staff morale. Allegedly, IBM employees referred to the Roadmap as 'Roadkill', as executives shifted technical expertise from high-paid US staff to low-salaried staff in India.[10] Managers, it has been alleged, were required to cull a certain percentage of their staff, regardless of an individual's absolute performance. With a reduced headcount those employees lucky enough to keep their jobs bear the brunt of increased workloads, covering the job demands left by their redundant co-workers. The wider company impact on returning dividends may also have impacted on the company's capacity to compete: for example, IBM failed to win a bid for the Central Intelligence Agency's lucrative cloud computing contract. Although its bid was said to be 30 per cent lower than that of Amazon's – which won the bid despite having no experience with government contracts – the IBM proposal was rejected on technical grounds.

This story is striking for several reasons. What it suggests is that unleashing finance has enormously increased the power of mobile capital owners in pursuit of short-term profits and high dividends. The surest way to deliver short-run profits is to minimise long-term investments, such as in machinery and research and development. Where short-term 'shareholder maximisation'[11] dominates business organisation then use of downsizing, outsourcing and offshoring often becomes the first, rather than the last, resort for management executives. Selling off less profitable parts of the business or sacking workers is often a quick fix for improving profit margins, boosting quarterly profits and increasing share price. Interestingly some recent studies have documented a link between 'shareholder maximisation' strategies and employment loss – see the very useful paper by Batt and Applebaum (2013) for a review. Shareholders have tended to encourage such behaviour by paying very high salaries to chief executives who are good at making cuts, even though, as with IBM, this may weaken the growth prospects of the company in the long run or, as with the General Motors example earlier, the race to seek new financial investments can lead to sudden corporate collapse. But of course shareholders do not necessarily care about the long-term future of the companies they invest in, for they can always sell their shares in pursuit of higher returns elsewhere. Indeed, as in the movie *Wall Street*, the very worst elements of shareholders who lack an interest are evident in Gekko's plans to liquate an airline and its workforce, asset strip its hanger division, peddle the manufacturing premises to property developers and sell its planes to Mexicans, whilst also raiding the workers' pension fund.

When questioned about the consequences of such actions for the company's workforce, he replies that 'it's all about the buck'.[12]

As the IBM tale demonstrates, employees often have to live with the serious consequences of the decisions emanating from far removed corporate investors whose only engagement with the company is through the arm's length interrogation of earnings on stock market indexes. So cost cutting, insecurity and job loss, even when the company seems to be performing pretty well, is the rather dark side of financialisation that employees face. As you can imagine, this creates a whole host of problems for HR departments in trying to generate highly committed and motivated individuals at work. For those subjected to the vagaries of shareholder demands, it erodes the ability to sustain high-trust relationships at work between employers and employees (Cushen and Thompson, 2016). Employees observe and experience that tension, resulting in growing disengagement from their employer, even if they continue, under the discipline of insecurity and fear of job loss, to offer high levels of effort. As one (former) Dean of Saïd Business School at Oxford University said:

> [Financialisation] systematically extinguishes any sense of commitment – of investors to companies, of executives to employees, of employees to firms, of firms to their investors, of firms to communities, or of this generation to any subsequent or past one. It is a transactional island in which you are as good as your last deal, as farsighted as the next deal, admired for what you can get away with, and condemned for what you confess. (Mayer, 2013[13])

The interaction between financialisation and workplace outcomes can play out in other ways. As Costas Lapavitsas (2012a; 2013) has recounted, the growing financialisation of economies is intimately linked to the dynamics of employment relations. The Eurozone offers a serviceable illustration. Prior to the creation of European Economic and Monetary Union (EMU), Germany's big exporters and employers, like Siemens, Daimler, Volkswagen, and ThyssenKrupp could rely on the Deutsche Bundesbank to devalue the mark to make their goods more competitive in international markets. Signing up to the single European currency clearly ruled this option out, so German employers were forced to redirect their energies to internal devaluations. In effect, this meant reducing the value of labour costs. Volkswagen was in the vanguard of this new approach. It adopted the 5000X5000 project at its Wolfsburg plant in 2001 which recruited new staff on lower terms and conditions than the company works council had previously agreed for existing workers (Schmidt and Williams, 2002). Meanwhile at national level the 'Hartz Reforms', named after Peter Hartz, the HR executive at Volkswagen who designed the policies,[14] eliminated payroll taxes on earnings of less than €400 a month, encouraging the creation of low-paying, part-time work (or what Germans call 'mini-jobs'). While the reforms probably ended up costing the ruling Social Democratic Party the next election, they gave employers an incentive to create lower paid (mini) jobs which at the same time 'encouraged' (or, perhaps, 'coerced') the unemployed to take them (Mitlacher, 2007). Fear of low benefits if you became unemployed, along with the threat of moving businesses abroad, combined to force German workers to accept very low wage increases.

German export manufacturers became comparatively efficient in areas such as machine tooling, chemicals and car production, which all generated vast trade surpluses that other peripheral Eurozone countries had been unable to compete with. Greece, for example, sucked in German exports that resulted in a massive domestic trade deficit (e.g. they were importing more than they were exporting). The gap was bridged by relying on financial borrowing from the likes of German and other European banks. Resting in German bank accounts, the surpluses accrued from wage repression at home were then recycled as loans across the wider Eurozone to governments. Yet when borrowing rates shot up in the aftermath of the 2008 Financial Crisis, debtor countries like Greece could no longer cover their repayments to core banks. To ensure payment, EU authorities, along with the International Monetary Fund, provided the Greek government with assistance loans to help repay the debt. In exchange, the Greeks were required to implement measures to get government spending down and boost competitiveness, including cuts in public sector wages, public sector employment, social welfare and state pensions alongside tax rises, privatisation and the reform of collective bargaining and employee dismissal laws. Similar dynamics have played out in other EU member countries, as core banking institutions have been protected at the expense of severe employment relations restructuring in peripheral states (for a review of ER reforms in these countries see Koukiadaki et al., 2016).

One final way we might consider the impact of financialisation is by returning to the aforementioned problem of stagnant wages as brought about by global capital mobility. It is sometimes forgotten that wages are not just as a cost, but are also a source of demand. Dampening wages can lead to a problem of unrealised demand: workers who get less, spend less. To resolve this problem, the credit economy became pretty important in plugging the gap between what labour was earning and what it could spend. Again, Lapavitsas (2012b: 34) argues that:

in financialised capitalism ordinary working people have come increasingly within the purview of the financial system...as social provision has retreated in the fields of housing, pensions, education and so on. To obtain basic goods...more individuals have been forced to rely on financial institutions.

This 'privatised Keynesianism', as Colin Crouch (2009) has termed it, meant that as real incomes of workers were not keeping pace with the cost of living, household debt financed much of their spending. Mortgage debt was and is a big chunk of this debt. But also as working families increasingly needed two cars to enable multiple members to do paid work, car loans became important components of household debt. But of course one person's debt is another's asset. The rise of indebted households provided employers and other finance speculators with a superb double opportunity. Imagine you are a General Motors executive in the United States in the 2000s. Not only are your workers' wages now suppressed for fear of losing their jobs to the Mexicans, but through your mortgage division you provide loans to these same workers who then pay you back from their stagnant wages, at a rate of interest. In some way workers, like investors, were engaging in speculative asset purchasing: houses became not so much a home to live in but an asset bought on cheap credit. More borrowing to buy homes increased demand for them and thus their prices. As prices rose, workers could refinance their homes and borrow more against the increased collateral their rising house values represented. And so the cycle continued, encouraged by government policies and large banks; that is, until it all collapsed of course.

Of related relevance is that employment relations within these banks and mortgage companies were often crucial to this dynamic: senior managers pushed their sales staff to sell more and more financial services or products to customers, with performance appraisal systems monitoring employee effort through the setting of sales targets. Customers in turn were encouraged by target-pressurised workers to take on loans, even if their suitability for such loans was dubious. Ultimately, the mortgage market, in countries like the United States, Spain, Britain and Ireland became particularly lucrative. In Ireland, for example, mortgage debt soared to as much as 180 per cent above the average wage during its Celtic Tiger boom years (McDonough and Dundon, 2010). In the United States the sub-prime market offered mortgages to workers on low and insecure incomes, which fuelled rising debt. Being high risk meant profits could be made if such workers managed to pay back their loans, but even if they failed banks could always repossess such homes whose values seemed in an inexorable rise upward. It meant, for employers and speculators, profit could be made either way.

crises and cutbacks

The unfortunate yet inevitable fact with all bubbles is, of course, they burst. The particular problem at the heart of the mortgage frenzy of the 2000s was that the rising assets, say house prices, derived from the intense competition amongst lenders to lend. An increase in the inability of workers to pay back their loans would result in a glut of houses onto the market, generating unpaid debts and eventually leading to house (asset) price reductions. This is of course what happened. As the market began to collapse, global financial institutions went into crisis; some were forced into mergers to survive, some went bankrupt, whilst others deemed 'too big to fail' had to be bailed out, nationalised or have their bad loans guaranteed with taxpayers' money. As the now bad loans had been distributed across numerous institutional investors, lenders became defensive, no one would lend and the market for credit 'crunched'. Consumer confidence sagged, housing construction ceased, demand imploded, retail sales plunged, redundancies and unemployment surged, and stores and manufacturing plants closed down or workers were put on short time. General Motors, for example, was declared bankrupt, mostly because it had diverted revenue into finance ventures and suffered substantial losses in sub-prime mortgage investments (Rubery, 2015). To survive, employment restructuring and concession bargaining, alongside a generous government bailout, would become the norm at GM in the USA (and abroad). Having taken on the debts of the banking system, many governments around the world found it increasingly difficult to cope and meet their own obligations. In some cases, a combination of bank debt guarantees and bailouts alongside a recessionary decline in tax receipts and a rise in welfare support pushed many countries' national debt skyward. Government austerity and the curbing of public spending ensued with all that has meant for employment relations, both in the public *and* private sector (Hudson, 2015).

If of course you are reflecting critically on all this you might note that when economies crash, big employers and particularly big banks that get hit worst are provided with bailouts and stimuli. Indeed, citizens' bailouts of the financial system's bad loans in this period seem to have demonstrated the limits of 'neo-liberalism' as policy practice. In neo-liberal theory, reckless investments in a market system should be punished by losses to the lender; but governments, in practice, actually made lenders relatively immune to such losses through a form of 'bad debt socialism'. While invariably designed to keep the financial system afloat and ensure credit, endeavours of this sort can actually be damaging to market discipline and market rationality by fostering 'moral hazard'. Thus financial investors, now too big to fail, realise that they will be bailed out come what may. If their debtors go bankrupt and cannot pay, national or supranational state power can be used to 'structurally adjust' said borrower until such time as they do cough up (if they ever do). Aside from the serious social dislocation such behaviours engender, it also encourages financiers to take on bigger risks than they might otherwise have done. As Philip Mirowski (2014) demonstrates, the roulette wheel at the casino spins on but only with the increasing risk of coming unstuck. Far from neo-liberal theory, such conditions might well suggest that actually existing capitalism is more akin to the rent-seeking activities of feudal barons.

At the same time business and large employers in the main tend to be averse to new taxes on them to pay for stimulus and bailout programmes. Governments that do raise taxes on business risk capital flight with all the inevitable consequences that has on tax receipts. So instead, governments turn to borrowing the necessary funds. Certainly, bailing out banks, other financial companies and selected corporations (in the auto industry for example) requires heavy borrowing. Yet those corporations, like insurance companies, mutual funds and large banks, used the money they saved by keeping governments from taxing them to provide the huge loans governments actually need. In contrast, the majority of middle- and lower-income workers lend little if anything to their governments, with transfers of incomes simply coming in the form of tax deductions from salaries and wages. Like the General Motors mortgage example earlier, corporations in this case substitute loans to the government instead of paying more in taxes. For those loans, governments pay interest. So government borrowing rewards corporations. Yet this arrangement raises a new problem. Where will governments find funds to both pay the interest on all the borrowing and pay back lenders the full sums borrowed? Government borrowing thus paradoxically becomes a problem for corporations who now worry that they might now see taxes hiked to help government pay back loans. In the face of a tax threat, employers threaten capital flight and investment strikes. Unable to tax corporations, austerity now becomes the alternative policy preferred by governments and of course some corporations. To reduce the deficit requires tax rises on workers incomes and government cuts to public sector employment, social services and welfare payments (Blyth, 2015). The money from those raised taxes and the savings from cuts is then used to pay interest on the national debt and reduce it over time. One might be tempted to reflect cynically on this method of resolving economic crises. For all the complexity and jargon of financial economics, for the layman it can often seem that such strategies amounts to little else than shifting the burden of adjustment, whether in the form of a bailout or later austerity, onto the backs of middle- and lower-income workers (Wolff, 2013).

As the image in Exhibit Box 3.2 below illustrates, those workers, now squeezed by falling living standards and angry that the executives of bailout banks continue to go on being well rewarded, march out on protest where they are usually shepherded by a police force who themselves are victims of the new financialisation of capitalism.

Exhibit Box 3.2   Financialisation and re-investment of public sector employee assets.

Credit: Mark Hurwitt, www.hurwittgraphics.com

As also implied by the image, the most powerful, the chief architects of our global financial system, remain relatively unscathed by crises of their making and continue to be rewarded with high salaries and bonus payments. Perhaps this is because, as Gordon Gekko notes in the movie *Wall Street*, referring to himself and his class of financiers:

> We make the rules, pal...We pick that rabbit out of the hat while everybody sits out there wondering how the hell we did it. Now, you're not naive enough to think we're living in a democracy, are you, buddy?

conclusion

So it is this context of casino-style speculation, crises and cutbacks that provides the dominant backdrop to contemporary employment relations in our times. Perhaps an overriding theme of our discussion is that ER are not hermetically sealed from the rest of the world's affairs. Although we have avoided discrete categorisations explicitly listing off how politics, law or markets act as environmental influences on employment relations, all of these influences nonetheless can be seen to permeate the considerations of this chapter. We have seen, at times through the eyes of Gordon Gekko, how the political economy of finance, debt and crises is intimately related to contemporary employment relations. In doing this we hope that you will take from our account that sometimes issues which appear to be remote from the academic concerns of employment relations, like say indebted households or the British chancellor's budget plans, can be quite central to the study of ER and work-related changes in an organisation or a society. Contrary to what some professional managerial associations might tell you, employment relations is a lot more than simply learning about the organisational-level employment relations processes that support organisational performance. Rather, ER is about society, politics and the economy, as well as inequality, ideology, power and privilege. Indeed in the pages that follow, it is these themes that will resurface.

4

Who's Who in Employment Relations?

You may have been fortunate enough to come across the British film *if....*, a stylised account of life in an all-boys public school in the mid-1960s. Charting the progress of the student body as they return for a new term, the film progressively reveals how authority, hierarchy and tradition shape school life. Whilst 'College', as it is known, is overseen by a headmaster, he remains something of a background figure, aloof from the boys and intervening infrequently to encourage their adherence to the 'traditions' of school life. From the boys' perspective, most of their daily experiences are shaped not by the headmaster or teachers, but by the 'Whips', upper-sixth-form pupils who have authority to act as 'prefect' over the other boys. Delegated to enforce 'house rules', this the Whips do capriciously, distributing rewards (toasted scones) and punishment (cold showers) when and as they see fit. Some Whips are austere and remote, others paternalistic. When the Whips are not enforcing 'rules', they make speeches to the lower forms advising attendance at school rugby matches and castigating prior displays of poor team spirit. Progressively the arbitrary treatment by the Whips, encourages three lower-sixth-formers to increasingly disengage from school life. Soon their clashes with school authorities and Whips become more and more contentious and finally a brutal caning by the latter transforms the boys' latent hostility into collectively organised resistance. For the Whips, the three non-conformers are seen as 'degenerates', dangerous subversives of college traditions. The school head is somewhat more measured: he views the boys' resistance as understandable but misguided and he is keen to curb both the worst excesses of the Whips and the recalcitrance of the boys in the interest of maintaining order. The film concludes precisely when the lower-sixth-formers undertake their ultimate act of resistance: at an end of term school event, they start a fire under the assembly hall, smoke everyone out, before proceeding to open fire from the rooftop with machine guns previously unearthed in a college attic.

You might wonder why we have begun a chapter on actors in employment relations by recounting the plot of a celebrated film from the 1960s, set in a boys' public school, and incidentally one of former British Prime Minister David Cameron's favourite movies.[15] In many ways, the film provocatively reflects the fundamental dynamics that exist between the main actors in employment relations, employers, workers and the state. It captures different ER perspectives discussed in Chapter 2, namely the 'unitarism' of presumed shared interests among different groups; a 'plurality' in accommodating divergent views among employment actors; and also 'radical' schools of thought in terms of acts of resistance against obtuse exploitation. There is some evidence that the film's director, Lindsay Anderson, intended the headmaster to reflect the post-war reformist state in Britain. Mirroring the headmaster, the British state, like many other 'Anglo-Saxon' societies, has historically remained detached from the day-to-day conduct of employment relations, preferring a policy which encouraged employers and workers to voluntarily conclude their own arrangements (Howell, 2007). However, at different times, to different degrees and to different effects, the state has intervened when quarrels between the other employment actors have strayed from 'socially tolerable' grounds. From the perspective of the government, such quarrels might well be legitimate, but they should not disrupt the normal working of society. Thus the state's authoritative voice is needed to maintain industrial peace, to exhort and regulate both employers and employees. The Whips, on the other hand, echo in some measure managers: they oversee and direct the students – who mimic the role of workers – on an everyday basis. Like the Whips, conformance with employer requirements is rewarded and transgressions are subject to discipline. In most cases, these hierarchical relations of control carry on uninterrupted: those at the top issue orders and oversee their execution whilst those at the bottom follow, obey and simultaneously often feel aggrieved. Much like life within the school, the majority of lower-form pupils within the hierarchy consent, albeit to different degrees and for a variety of reasons, to the expectations and orders transmitted from above. Yet, as in *if....*, the relationship between the higher and lower echelons of the hierarchy can become strained. The pupils do protest, resist and seek to exercise counter-control over the hierarchical relations. True, most workers will never, unlike the boys, take to arms, and opposition will be peaceful, although in 2012 striking South African miners armed with machetes did engage in pitched battle with police at the Lonmin platinum mines in a strike over pay.[16] Nonetheless, for many employers, challenges of any sort are typically unwelcome: employers, like the Whips, are likely to regard such resistance, in true unitary fashion, as based on flawed understandings or to be the product of troublemakers (Fox, 1966).

In college, the different actors perform their respective roles in ways that are conditioned and related to each other. Although none can exist without the other, each of the actors has somewhat different interests: realising these requires interaction with the others, producing various patterns and outcomes. Similarly, in the field of ER, actors like employers, workers and the state pursue their own interests, but which in realisation also demand interaction and co-dependency producing different behaviours that can range from cooperation to conflict. Moving beyond our introductory analogy, we will now flesh out the roles of these different actors, of employers, workers and the state. Our intention is essentially to give a flavour of what these actors do in the employment relationship and why they do what they do.

the employer

Let us begin our account of employers by imagining for a moment that out there in the world is an individual called Rockefeller. A man of good fortune, Rockefeller happens to hold claim to a significant stock of money. How he acquired such money is, for our purposes, unimportant. Of more significance is that Rockefeller is eager to expand his money stock and accumulate further wealth. If Rockefeller was like a growing number of his contemporaries, he might follow the financialisation trends we discussed in the previous chapter and invest his stock in financial markets, attempt to profit on fluctuating commodity values, or speculate in Greek government debt. Our Rockefeller, however, has a keen interest in creating wealth through the production of useful goods. He has spotted a gap in the market for widget manufacture, and has decided that his future lies in widget production. To fulfil his ambitions, this aspiring manufacturer begins trading under the brand Widget Inc., using his money to purchase the necessary tools and machinery for widget assembly, source raw materials and a site for production. Yet something remains incomplete: whilst admiring the new machinery on the floor of his new factory, Rockefeller realises his investments hitherto will come to nought unless some hands are put to transforming its productive potential into saleable widgets. Whilst he knows much about the potential market for widgets, he knows little of the skilled craft that is demanded for widget production. Rockefeller requires labour and must therefore enter the abode of the labour market to secure what he needs.

The labour market is not unproblematic to the prospective buyer of labour (Purdy, 1988). Much will depend on the time and location at which Rockefeller enters its ambit and the kind of labour and skill set he seeks. If Rockefeller should enter at a period of full employment when jobs are plentiful, he may find it difficult to secure the kind of labour he needs, as either the pool of unemployed labour reserves do not exist or other firms, keen to meet their order books, are competing with him to hire workers. Widget production is a highly skilled trade requiring years of apprenticeship and craft tutelage; consequently, Rockefeller might find it difficult to source that quality of worker with ease. By all accounts the labour market has been an endemic problem for many buyers of labour along China's coastal cities in recent years, with labour shortages resulting in costly wage inflation as firms bid to attract and retain workers. In some cases the shortages have been so intense and the wage inflation so high as to encourage Chinese firms to relocate abroad or circumvent their reliance on human labour by auto-mating production processes.[17] Even the calibre of candidates in the local labour market may concern Rockefeller. Upon building assembly plants in Brazil, Volkswagen opted to locate its factory in the agricul-tural Resende region rather than the traditional industrialised areas of Sao Paulo. Whilst local government tax breaks were part of the story, it also stemmed from the comparative nature of the labour markets in the two regions. The German employer, well known for its pro-unionism and worker participation at home, did not want to rely on Sao Paolo workers with their traditions of union organisation and militancy: they thought it in their own vested interests to locate in an agricultural region of high unemployment, ensuring access to a willing workforce with little union experience (Ramalho and Francisco, 2008).

Fortunately for Rockefeller, his local labour market is marked by high levels of unemployment and is awash with eager sellers (workers) of labour. Rockefeller settles on one person (as that is all we'll assume he needs at present), a Mr Kunz, and agrees with him the various particulars of what is required. The terms of the employment contract are such that in exchange for payment, Mr Kunz promises to work under the direction of Rockefeller, now his employer, for a designated number of hours every week as long as required. Furthermore, the terms and conditions of employment specify Kunz's job description, work rules and operating procedures, written exclusively by Rockefeller and presented to Kunz and is signed by the parties. Rockefeller can thus set Mr Kunz to work under his directed authority and allow production at Widget Inc. to begin.

All is fine with this arrangement until, over time, Rockefeller begins to realise that the agreement with Kunz is not as straightforward as first expected. Rockefeller has on occasion spied Kunz on the factory floor working at a pace far from what his employer thinks is possible. At other times, Mr Kunz has been observed loading the widget machine in a way that Rockefeller regards as unnecessarily time consuming and inefficient. Rockefeller has discovered that no matter how detailed a contract is, difficulties emerge in specifying in advance how much work, and of what sort, shall be expended, at what time and in what way, for a given wage. The commodity of labour, sold by Kunz, is distinct because what is being bought and sold are human mental and physical capacities and not Mars bars, tins of soup or iPhones. There is always a measure of uncertainty or indeterminacy about the conditions of such an ongoing exchange (Smith, 2006). At best, Rockefeller has purchased a promise to work, but that potential has still to be secured in everyday production through the use of monitoring, exhortation and various other means of control and surveillance. Rockefeller must consume the labour power he has purchased, for otherwise his investment will not amount to much.

Even more pressing for Rockefeller, as an employer, is the fact that new firms have entered the widget production market, some of whom appear to be producing more at much less cost than Widget Inc. Compelled to lower unit labour costs, Rockefeller remonstrates with his new hire on several occasions, cajoling and chastising Kunz to raise his productivity. Whilst Rockefeller plays with the idea of sacking Mr Kunz, the fortunes of the local labour market have turned since recruiting him and it is now much 'tighter'; securing, in a timely fashion, skilled labour qualified in the art of widget production will not be easy and would risk holding up production and losing orders to the competition. Mr Kunz's bargaining position has shifted (temporarily) to his advantage, owing to labour market changes (Martin, 1992).

In any event, Rockefeller has limited time to deal with Kunz. Demands of the business flow from several sources and not just production, and his attention has turned elsewhere (negotiating cheaper suppliers). To ensure the product continues to roll off the line at Widget Inc. and that Kunz supplies a satisfactory amount of productive labour in his absence, Rockefeller hires a manager as an overseer of production. One Ms Sloan is appointed, and contracted, under a duty of stewardship, to protect and advance Rockefeller's business interests. In practice this provides Sloan with delegated formal authority over Kunz in order to direct his activities towards profitable ends for Widget Inc. Ms Sloan is effectively the agent acting as Rockefeller. But this is not an easy role for Ms Sloan. If Widget Inc. and thus Rockefeller's interests are not met, Ms Sloan will bear the brunt of the business owner's wrath. On the other hand, Sloan finds Kunz to be a tricky character who is sometimes unresponsive to requests to work harder. Mr Kunz seems to know he is not easily replaceable. A core issue for this new manager is how the less-than-ideal Kunz will fully submit to the authority of management. Sloan is likely to claim a right to command Kunz on several different grounds: first, given the devolved authority Sloan has been granted by the owner, she might argue that this empowers her with rights to dictate company resources. In the eyes of Sloan, Mr Kunz, whose labour time has been paid for, is regarded as a resource like any other resource the business might buy and use accordingly. Therefore Mr Kunz can be deployed, Sloan reasons, as management's needs require. Alternatively, if this alleged claim to some enshrined 'right' to deploy Kunz is too crude for a sophisticated manager like Ms Sloan, she might also rationalise her authority by pointing to her CIPD accredited postgraduate certificate from the prestigious ACME University School of Business. In other words, she has obtained a specialist business management qualification, which she claims is similar to that of a practising lawyer. Sloan uses this idea of a unique managerial skill set to argue that she alone has the requisite 'professional' competence to make decisions about how best to organise the work process in ways that the blue-collar Mr Kunz could never understand.

Assured in such reasoning, Ms Sloan proceeds to get the most profitable work she can out of Kunz and 'maximise' his potential labour output. To achieve this, Sloan has potentially several options. She may use her accredited knowledge to analyse Kunz's work patterns, parcelling out individual elements of his job task to unskilled workers. Ms Sloan may also introduce new technology that speeds up the 'cycle time' of Kunz's widget assembly. Alternatively, Sloan, immersed in the latest literature on some recent business fad such as 'global talent management', may experiment with methods designed to enrich Mr Kunz's experience of work in order to 'engage' him. Perhaps the payment system in place will be aligned to Mr Kunz's performance, quantity of his work, or quality of widgets produced, or may be linked to a share of company profits, a practice well established in the American firm Lincoln Electric, as detailed in Frank Koller's book *Spark* (2010). Either of the options Sloan adopts may also depend to a significant degree on what scholars of employment relations call 'management style' – that is, a preferred way of exercising authority and control over subordinates lower in the employment hierarchy (Purcell, 1987).

If we return to the analogy of school life, our prior discussion of how authority is exercised will be recalled. Philip Roscoe, author of the very engaging *I Spend, Therefore I Am* (2014), recounts his days at Berkhamsted, a private boys' school in the South of England and something akin to a modern-day version of the 'college' featured in *if.....* Roscoe gives his personal account of the 'whips' (prefects) who would require new pupils – the 'fags' – to run personal errands, but also engage them in acts of humiliation for the amusement of the whips. Roscoe recalls how a senior prefect 'commanded him to stand on his head and sing', subsequently unimpressed by his 'rendition of Rat in the Kitchen'. The experiences of one of the authors of this book at an alternative Liverpool comprehensive inner-city school is similar: instead of singing on one's head, informal (or unofficial) prefects would issue instructions to steal cigarettes and alcohol from a retail outlet for the purpose of furnishing the 'Cock of the Year' with personal supplies, or face the prospect of some (usually violent) bullying retributive act. A parallel variation in articulated styles and managerial behaviours is evident across organisations. Some managers will be brutish, bureaucratic and seek to tightly control their staff, whilst others will be informal and perhaps more considerate in their relations with employees. Other styles might be characterised by sophisticated management techniques, based around job enrichment and motivation, whilst others will encourage opportunities for negotiation, participation and co-determination. At a fundamental level, management style is a matter of particular ideological preference, but other numerous factors will intrude and shape the way managerial authority is exercised, from the nature and extent of competition in the sector and in the labour market, to customer demands, trade union power, government laws and regulations, company size and type of firm ownership (e.g. family-run business, public sector service, or large scale multinational, multisite corporation). For instance, the legal enactments of a particular country in which a firm is located will shape how employer authority is wielded. Imagine Ms Sloan did decide one day to just get rid of Mr Kunz. If Widget Inc. was based in Turin in Italy, Sloan would find that her ability to dismiss Kunz would be heavily restricted, with the requirement that strict bureaucratic formalities be followed before any dismissal take place. In contrast, were Widget Inc. located in the American state of Alabama, Ms Sloan would have absolute dismissal power; there would be no requirement to mention any reason for sacking Mr Kunz, nor would there be any need to comply with specific formalities. Poor Mr Kunz could be fired at will because his employer prefers that action on that particular day.

the worker

At this point it may be useful to turn our attention in more detail to Mr Kunz as a specific actor capable of influencing employment relations in his workplace. Kunz, as it so happens, is of very different origin and circumstance to Rockefeller. For a variety of reasons, he does not possess or have access to any significant stock of money and so cannot easily follow a similar path to Rockefeller in entering the world of business. What Kunz does possess is knowledge of a particular craft – that of the skilled machinist, an art he acquired from several years of training during his apprenticeship at a local technical college. Upon completion of his training, Kunz had aspired to continue this noble craft as a livelihood. However, to his dismay, Mr Kunz learnt that the raw materials, tools and machines he had so freely used in class each week were beyond his financial reach to purchase on the market. Lacking access to these resources, Kunz was left idle, neither able to practise his craft or make a living in the trade he had so assiduously mastered. Reliant on welfare benefits, Kunz spent much time at the local labour exchange, hoping to find an opportunity for work in his craft. Time was running out for Kunz: if he did not find a job in his chosen trade, his welfare administrator was pressuring him to take a position in the local *Poundland* store, or have his benefit stopped. Fortunately, as we know, a posting in his line of work turned up at Widget Inc., for which Mr Kunz successfully applied.

Over time however, the terms and conditions of his hire did not always match Kunz's original expectations. In the same way that the 'indeterminacy' of labour potential can work both for and against Rockefeller, it can also work both for and against Kunz. What this means for our immediate purpose is that Mr Kunz now finds the constant interruptions by Rockefeller and Sloan (the management) into his work not only irksome but that they are leading potentially to violation of his work role expectations. From Mr Kunz's perspective, the management seem to have no understanding or appreciation of good quality widget work and are more interested in churning out the product as quickly as possible. He feels that management constantly harangue him about 'inefficient' and 'slow' loading of the machine when, as Kunz points out, to load any faster would damage the component material.

Soon Ms Sloan has many of the old machines replaced with new imported technology, changing many of the tasks performed by Kunz: automated machines do most of the interesting skilled work and he is reduced to being something of a mere handler of the component feed (a task which he is nonetheless required to do, it seems, at an ever-increasing pace). Mr Kunz starts to resent management's arbitrary ways. Some days they tell Kunz to cut short lunch to return to work, whilst other days he is asked to do jobs which he did not believe he agreed to on signing the contract, like sweeping the factory floor before leaving for the day. Furthermore, with management's continual demand for a faster work pace, Mr Kunz is beginning to find the level of required effort increasingly beyond the limits of what he expected upon taking up employment. He seems to be providing – at progressively intolerable levels – much more labour than he initially believed he consented to (or indeed experienced) upon starting at Widget Inc. Surely this disparity between wages and effort needs to be balanced, he contends. And surely the company can afford to pay him more? After all, business appears to be booming, new assembly lines and a number of new hires have recently been added, observes Mr Kunz. Redress in Mr Kunz's eyes may seem a matter of common sense. However, evidence tends to show that such employee assumptions of what might be equitable can fall on deaf (managerial) ears. When Kunz attempts to raise his thoughts and concerns to management, he is given short shrift. 'If you don't like it here, there are plenty more people outside the factory gates we can replace you with', he is told. Things do not look good for Mr Kunz.

Curiously, one day whilst eating his lunch beside his machine (there is no canteen at Widget Inc.), Kunz looks around the hive of activity that is the factory floor and observes his individual co-workers bustling away at their machines. They too, Kunz knows, are experiencing much the same treatment at Widget Inc. In the staff changing rooms he has heard them curse their luck over shortened lunch breaks, faster work pace and arbitrary treatment. He knows too of those that have raised their objections with Ms Sloan, only to be told much the same as he was: 'If you don't like it here, there are plenty more people outside the factory gates we can replace you with.' Then it slowly dawns upon Kunz's consciousness: true, he might be easily replaced by the management, as indeed might any other one of the individual workers he shares the factory floor with. But could management easily replace all of them? And at the same time? Might not their voice as employees of Widget Inc. be heard more loudly if they spoke in unison?

Mr Kunz realises that speaking collectively does not necessarily mean their voice is effectively or automatically heard. He is well aware that many individuals with shared interests in society speak collectively as one, with various degrees of success or relevance: the Anarchist Federation, the Organization of the Petroleum Exporting Countries (OPEC), British Medical Association, Surfers Against Sewage and RANGA (Red and Nearly Ginger Association). What is it that the oil sheiks have that, say, the 'ginger haired' folk don't? It seems, Mr Kunz thinks, that what makes the difference between whether one group gets heard or not, is that, apart from acting collectively, they can also exercise or mobilise *power* to leverage their agenda and interest. At the risk of upsetting many sophisticated political philosophers (Lukes, 2005), *power* in this context might be expressed simply where 'A' (workers at Widget Inc.) has the capacity to get 'B' (management of Widget Inc.) to do something that 'B' would otherwise prefer not to do (pay the workers at Widget Inc. more money). It follows that for collective power to be mobilised in this way, the workers of Widget Inc. must be able to threaten, or actually impose, some sanction, and one of sufficient intensity, to get management to listen and hopefully address the workers' concerns.

Kunz is now deep in thought: what capacity to exercise power might the workers at Widget Inc. possess, he ponders? He knows, for example, that the power of OPEC stems from their control over the supply of oil. If oil-importing countries do something that OPEC dislike, OPEC can curb supplies and raise the prize of a barrel of oil. For OPEC, oil is thus their crucial, in-demand resource. In contrast, red-heads (e.g. RANGA) have no such in-demand collective power resource. Mr Kunz is now alive to the possibilities: collectively, the workers at Widget Inc. are the sellers of labour power to Rockefeller, the buyer of their capacity to work, on a day-to-day basis. Should this supply of labour be cut short or stymied in some way, production could stutter, widgets are unmade, orders get unrealised and the money which flows into Widget Inc. from customer purchases dries up. The collective supply of labour effort is thus the Widget Inc. workers' power resource: it can be used as retaliatory action in pursuing the workers' aims and interests, which can and often do differ from those of management.

In some respects, Mr Kunz is now thinking like an investor. When Rockefeller invests his money into widget production, it seems only reasonable for Rockefeller to continue his investment if the return is satisfactory. It would seem irrational for Rockefeller to continue to invest his main resource, that is his money on widget production, should the anticipated rewards be inadequate. Rather, until the conditions are right, Rockefeller might easily go on an investment strike. Similarly, Kunz reasons that when he invests his labour power (a commodity on the labour market), why should he continue this investment, his supply of labour, if what he receives in return, the rewards from work, do not merit continued labour 'investment'? Of course, Mr Kunz is not an equal investor in the same way or at the same level as Rockefeller. Kunz is an individual worker: he has little alternative but to sell his capacity to labour at the best price (wage) he can get (offered by management). Recall he was almost forced to work in *Poundland* or have his benefits stopped, but for the timely set-up of Widget Inc. But part of Mr Kunz's thinking is he has now observed that management at Widget Inc. often reduce production output in a bid to create artificial shortages, thereby boosting prices on the market. If their employer can do it, why not the workers as a collective force at Widget Inc.? The possibility of a labour strike can be a rational worker response to counterbalance the excesses of managerial power and protect or advance employee interests.

In reality there are likely to be a good many workers who supply their labour on terms that they feel have become unsatisfactory, but for various reasons (lack of power, management pressure, etc.) find it difficult to withdraw their labour resource. This is why Kunz's realisation of labour 'power' is so significant. Through combination and union, the resource of 'collective labour power' can be used to regulate the relations between workers and the employer. They can present their demands on wages and conditions of employment with the aim of collectively bargaining more effectively than they ever could do as separate individuals, and, in relative terms, be easily replaceable when acting separately. It would be quite difficult for Ms Sloan to displace the whole workforce at Widget Inc. (albeit not impossible). Indeed, it was this awareness amongst many industrialised workers globally in the 19th and 20th centuries that encouraged the widespread growth of trade unionism.

To turn these bold ambitions into reality, Mr Kunz realises that he and his co-workers must organise. But this will be no easy task. The embryonic collective may encounter statutory laws which prohibit individuals combining independently to alter the terms and conditions of their employment in ways that improve their lot, at a cost to the employer. Since the 1980s, government laws in Britain have made it more and more difficult to organise collectively into trade unions to campaign or take action. While some co-workers rally to the cause and begin to mobilise, they can find it difficult convincing individuals that any proposed action will be effective. Some will be sceptical, perhaps believing they stand a better chance on their own. Some workers may secretly hope to gain from the struggles of those prepared to challenge employers. These are the 'free riders' who take the gains and benefits yet refrain from joining or acting in solidarity. Some of Mr Kunz's contemporaries may also genuinely fear for the consequences of being seen to act in a way that might challenge management. Indeed Ms Sloan, who has got an inkling of what is happening on the shop floor, has already raised objections to the workforce in a company briefing, declaring that unionisation will be seen by Rockefeller as an act of betrayal or disloyalty. In such circumstances, considerable resolve and effort will be needed to raise the collective consciousness of individual workers. This might involve identifying how individual employees share interests with a broader class of other similar workers, both at Widget Inc. but also across an industry, sector or even nationally. There have been strong campaigns in the past to raise the collective consciousness among employees internationally: 'workers of the world unite'. Specifically, workers (and their unions) might need to emphasise how interests on wages and effort differ from those of the employer and that such differences might only be remedied through collective action. Getting Mr Kunz and his co-workers to collectively identify shared interest amongst themselves is not easy, requiring much effort and persuasion on the part of the core organisers (for a classic example of this see Batstone et al., 1978).

An analogy to consider the discussion further is the Simpsons episode, 'Last Exit to Springfield'. In this episode Homer is (accidentally) elected as the President of the Union Brotherhood of Nuclear Technicians and Pastry Chefs. In the scene the factory owner, Mr Burns, attempts to eliminate a generous employee dental package from an existing collective agreement. Burns' encouragement for this is to offer a keg of free Duff beer for the workers at all company briefings. Whilst at first many of the plant workers are keen to accept the company's dangled carrot, it is only the intervention of Homer, who convinces his colleagues of the potential folly of conceding their dental benefit, which was hard fought for during the big strike of '88. Although Lenny, Carl and Gummy-Joe undoubtedly have a preference for free beer, perhaps even more so during working hours, they also have an interest in the dental benefit. Their interests are evidently opposite to the interests of the employer, Mr Burns, who seeks cost savings by removing the dental plan from the plant employees' terms and conditions. In his (surprising) role as an informal workplace leader, Homer has to identify and in turn convince workers of what seems to be their best interest, ensuring he can bring enough of them together collectively to persuasively withstand company pressure and counter-propose a solution. Homer succeeds and collective mobilisation forces Burns to retreat and renegotiate the dental plan for all.

However, the reality is that there are often so many difficulties for workers to organise themselves collectively that it is surprising that they ever form trade unions at all. Yet since the 19th century workers across many economies have achieved this, building up sizeable collective organisations of labour unions operating across plants, companies, sectors and even as national actors. Interestingly this has encouraged employers to do the same to counter collective worker power, by creating employer groups, associations and federations.

the state

In turning to our third actor in employment relations, we are not dealing with a particular, identifiable agent that we can personify in the same way as with Rockefeller the employer, Ms Sloan the manager, or Mr Kunz our employee contemplating unionisation. To do this with the state would be difficult because it is not so much an identifiable individual but rather an assemblage of different institutions – the elected government, the judiciary, the civil service and governmental departments, the police and many other agencies of the state (Jessop, 1990). Most conventional textbooks on employment relations will equate the elected government of the day with other agencies of the state that carry out its will and implement its legislation. Whilst the government of the day is clearly an important actor in employment relations, the 'other agencies of the state' in and of themselves are important not just as compliant actors within or part of the state, but are often important and influential in terms of their own autonomous actions (Barrow, 1993). Here we might think of the likes of senior civil servant mandarins advising government ministers, high court judges making legislative decisions (for example, issuing an injunction overnight to stop Mr Kunz and his co-workers commencing a strike at Widget Inc.), or even secret services. It can be misleading to assume these agencies of the state are somehow empty vessels or neutral players geared only to support and transmit government policy. It can be argued that the actors within the discrete state agencies act in ways that are highly independent and driven by their own rationales and logic. Indeed at various times, these different state actors – from the government to the police and the military – have all played an important role in shaping relations between the key employment actors like Rockefeller, Sloan and Kunz (see for example Peak, 1984; Geary, 1985).

Turning to another short analogy may serve to illustrate the argument, even help personalise the logic and power of state agencies. In the seminal BBC TV series *Yes Minister*, in the episode 'The Compassionate Society', the role and influence of governmental (state) actors on employment relations come to the fore. The episode commences with the Minister for Administrative Affairs, Mr Jim Hacker, expressing concern to his senior civil servant, the mandarin Sir Humphrey Appleby, for 'juggling the figures' to show a reduction in administrative staff in the public sector. Sir Humphrey reclassified data-processing operatives as 'technical' staff, and the minister incorrectly reported a reduction of around 11 per cent in the number of administrative staff. When criticising Sir Humphrey for reducing only the figures and not the number of actual administrators, Sir Humphrey lambasts the minister for not being clear and specific enough, 'You only asked for a reduction in the figures, not the number of administrators.'

In relation to employment relations matters, the episode gets even better. After Hacker's chauffeur, George, explains that a new hospital, St Edward's, has opened with over 500 staff but no patients, the minister sets his junior civil servant, Bernard, to investigate the situation. Bernard explains that St Edward's Hospital is fully staffed with administrators and ancillary workers, but owing to government cutbacks there was no funding left for medical treatment. Aware that his minister is investigating the issue, Sir Humphrey decides to meet for an informal drink with his counterpart, Sir Ian Whitchurch, the mandarin civil servant to the Minister for Health. Sir Ian explains that the government could not open a new hospital and start running it with patients straight away, 'There aren't any nurses yet... there might be in 18 months or so... possibly... if funds are available... possibly.' Sir Ian subsequently points out that the unions won't like the idea of a fully operational hospital within such a timeframe. The two senior civil servants conspire to transfer a militant 'firebrand' shop steward, Billy Fraser, from elsewhere in the NHS to St Edward's Hospital, knowing he will oppose Minister Hacker's plans. Sir Humphrey subsequently follows up and meets Brian Baker, the national union leader for the sector. At first Baker can find little argument to object to Hacker's plan. However Sir Humphrey, with eloquence of persuasion, convinces Brian Becker that a strong case could be made if industrial action was threatened, then all administrative and ancillary workers' jobs could be saved, even though the hospital had no patients, at least not yet.

Hacker visits the hospital, declares that 300 workers must go unless patients are admitted. In response Bill Fraser, the union shop steward, calls a strike. Minister Hacker calls his bluff, assuming a strike will have no impact as there are no patients to disrupt. Indeed, Hacker is self-congratulatory and enjoys a drink back in his ministerial office with Bernard, only to be shocked when Billy Fraser appears on the evening news announcing a large-scale strike across 'all' London hospitals. The Prime Minister is furious with Hacker. Fortuitously, a related political crisis presents itself: Cuban refugees are left homeless and face extradition from the United Kingdom. Hacker moves quickly and offers to house them using the beds in St Edward's Hospital, the strike is called off, the ancillary hospital workers retain their jobs and the refugees are supported by a 'compassionate state'.

Importantly, the wit and tongue-in-cheek humour of *Yes Minister* illustrates that state agencies may not in and of themselves act as empty vessels transmitting government ideals. Civil servants are clearly active agents who can influence government ministers. They may not directly determine specific legislation or government political values, yet they can influence and shape the posture of public policy on a range of areas, including employment relations. Likewise, workers such as Mr Kunz or Billy Frazer can, in turn, influence employers and the government about employment relations priorities.

The *Yes Minister* analogy is specifically public sector related. Some might suggest that these particular roles performed by the different agencies of the state function as a way of supporting both the stability and legitimacy of the employment relationship between Rockefeller and Kunz. This objective has numerous elements to it. For example, the state, through the court system, protects the private property rights of our employer, Rockefeller, and the sanctity of the employment contract. This enables Rockefeller to insist on his right to manage and extract profit from his employee, Mr Kunz. It also by necessity excludes Kunz from staking a claim over the assets used in Rockefeller's private sphere of production and the profits which ensue. Thus when in 2009 workers 'occupied' a Thomas Cook outlet in Dublin, protesting over being informed that they were to be laid off with immediate effect, the company turned to law and the court system, which granted an order for the arrest of the workers on the grounds that they had illegally seized private property. The order was duly carried out in a dawn raid by dozens of Irish police who, using battering rams to smash down the doors of the offices, arrested the workers and took them to a nearby station for questioning, before transferring them to the courts for sentencing.

It has been indicated that the state's role is to provide conditions and incentives that will induce the likes of Rockefeller to invest his monetary assets on an ongoing basis – that is, in a so-called 'pro-business environment'. In market societies, for politicians, economic growth and job creation anticipates that Rockefeller will make a profit which can then be taxed and used as a source of revenue to finance state activities (passing and maintaining laws, protecting nature reserves, providing lollipop ladies and so on). If the state fails in inducing Rockefeller to invest, not only will the lack of economic activity disrupt state finances but employment opportunities for the likes of Mr Kunz will become scarce. In circumstances of no investment and mass unemployment, not only will the state's finances become strained (through a decrease in revenue and increase in welfare expenditure), government will also have difficulty in reproducing that society in a stable and legitimate fashion. An unemployed Mr Kunz, with few employment or life prospects, may well question the legitimacy of a state and society which enables such conditions. He may become radicalised, resulting in revolution, perhaps even going as far as expropriating the unused productive assets from Rockefeller. How state agencies ensure a 'pro-business' environment is manifold: from offering competitive tax rates on his widget profits, providing infrastructural support like motorways and rail lines to transport his widgets to market, along with supporting educational interventions to improve labour force skill. For our purposes, however, we need only consider the contribution of employment relations in this respect, where even in this particular sphere we find multiple options – ranging from coercion to consent – for the government to assist the Rockefellers of this world in ensuring profitable investment in the economy. In very stark terms, Chile, under the repressive Pinochet regime, ensured high profits by using military force and secret police powers to limit workers' demands and crush independent trade unionism. More recently the International Trade Union Confederation has also claimed that the Colombian state is allowing right-wing paramilitary groups a free hand in intimidating and murdering labour activists, probably people not too dissimilar from our Mr Kunz, who may be seeking collective bargaining and unionisation to raise wages.[18] It is plausible, however, that state objectives and policies that lead to wage repression and union marginalisation to favour Rockefeller over Mr Kunz and his co-workers may be counter-productive in the long run: whilst firms may find they have lower production costs, they may also find that demand in the market dries up as workers with declining incomes buy fewer goods and services. We saw the dysfunctional consequences of this in Chapter 3.

There are many more plausible reasons to suggest that the prospects of maintaining a good business environment by crudely curbing the freedom and liberties of Mr Kunz or repressing his wages will not be successful. Such a ploy is likely to have little legitimacy for Kunz and his co-workers. It will probably fuel further resentment, hostility and resistance. A government of the day may find that that their prospects at the next election are bleak as the oppressed masses opt to vote for an alternative party, offering more favourable supports to Mr Kunz and his colleagues. Perhaps a combination of vote-conscious politicians and pressure from interest groups other than Rockefeller may dilute the appeal for a good business environment based exclusively on labour exclusion and suppression. Rather, the government will have to secure an appropriate balance between securing conditions for efficient profitable accumulation by Rockefeller, while meeting the needs of a broad range of social groups, like workers and citizens. Thus the state, either through its own social policy objectives or by being mindful of the electoral power of Kunz, is likely to protect workers from the worst excesses of employer power and the untrammelled pursuit of profit by establishing basic standards or rules of employment. Rubery and Grimshaw (2003) articulate the issue in terms of 'labour de-commodification'; that is, the extent to which a government provides social welfare protection so workers are not entirely exposed on the arbitrary whims of the free market and employer power. Of course, this need not be through purely calculative reasons of electoral advantage: many governments of a social-democratic and left-wing hue introduced such policies in the last century because of ideological commitment and because they were rooted in working class communities and trade union milieus (indeed the state often became a major employer itself as the scope of its activities in society expanded through welfare provision and administration). In any event, in democratic societies generally, social norms and expectations around fairness and justice have general support. Even when the most pro-business of political administrations introduces legislation that restricts or dilutes workers' rights, such actions will be presented as if they meet the general interests of all, demonstrating the significance of the state's need to secure some modicum of social legitimacy. Ultimately, then, whatever the source or motive, the rules and laws the state enact will likely seek to encourage 'stable' employment relations by specifying sanctions that can be taken against those who flout the rules or restrict or outlaw socially unpalatable practices.[19] If we return to our scenario depicted earlier, the state may be concerned about the disruption that may ensue should Kunz and his colleagues organise collectively and engage in strike action to pressurise Rockefeller to submit to their demands. Lost production and industrial militancy are general outcomes a government would prefer to avoid, for economic and social reasons. To overcome this potential, state agencies may encourage Kunz and Rockefeller to recognise the legitimacy of their respective interests and find ways to voluntarily reconcile their differences through peaceful negotiation and timely agreement. This might simply involve the state exhorting Rockefeller and Kunz to work together for the benefit of the nation. Alternatively, the state might take a more direct and active coordinating role, as has been the fashion in some European countries. Here the state may bring the parties to the table of government so to speak, providing them with a say over social and economic policy in exchange for moderation in the pursuit of their respective interests at national, industry and workplace level. In Austria, for example, trade unions, employers' organisations and state institutions play a key role in the governance of the employment relationship, particularly at national and regional level (Traxler, 1998).

Whichever route is taken by the state – from pro-market supports to alternative regimes advancing labour coordination and participation – will depend on a variety of different factors like motivation, political willingness and ideology, labour mobilisation and capacity. In simple terms we might say that in the example of Austria, the motivation to pursue the aforementioned policies partly stemmed from historical experiences of bitter class struggles and Nazis totalitarianism in the first half of the 20th century and a subsequent desire to move towards a social democratic consensus through a system of social partnership. Broadly similar patterns have evolved in a number of other European states (Crouch, 1993). In response to the pressures of globalisation, many of these more coordinated states are increasingly shifting the locus of exchange away from the centralised national bargaining to more decentralised systems of bargaining, like regional, sector or even company level. The process is sometimes called 'centrally coordinated decentralisation' or 'organised decentralisation' (Traxler, 2003). Rather than strong national or industry collective associations of Rockefeller and Mr Kunz negotiating the outcomes of the employment relationship, the trend is towards company-level bargaining. That this is occurring is because employers want to organise employment relations with maximum discretion and flexibility, justified as a necessary response to international competition. Where states cannot offer such environments of more flexible regulation and greater freedoms to the employer, the threat of investment loss and capital flight looms large, as we saw in the previous chapter. The ability of employers to switch capital to other states encourages governments to provide all sorts of incentives, like ensuring flexible systems of wage determination, to keep the Rockefellers of contemporary capitalism content. The result is often an increasingly smaller state with declining regulatory powers and an expansion in the private sphere of employer power.

conclusion

What we have reviewed in this chapter are the main activities or 'logics' of actor behaviour in employment relations, from the perspective of employer, workers and the state. Employers, like our Rockefeller, have to turn out profitable production and, in the main, require labour to do so. This they secure through the labour market, but only as a form of labour potential: they must squeeze that labour out in the process of production. This conversion problem, or effort bargain, entails a necessary interplay between employers and their hired workers revolving around potential combinations of conflict and cooperation. This is the structural anatagonism, referred to in Chapter 1, in action. We saw this same problem from the perspective of the individual worker. Different interests and struggles play out in the realm of rewards and degrees of acceptable effort between both parties: the employer, seeking to raise profits by keeping wages down and productivity up, whilst the worker seeks to maintain higher wages and supply labour in what they might regard as tolerable amounts. To recall our opening analogy of life at a school in *if....*, the different actors perform their respective roles in ways that are conditioned and related to each other. Although none can exist without the other, each of the actors has somewhat different interests. Yet realising these requires interaction with the others, producing various patterns and outcomes. Employers are likely to experiment with different patterns of control, ranging from crude or technocratic control mechanism to sophisticated engagement techniques. Workers are unlikely to be passive recipients and will attempt to wield some counter-control to protect and advance their own interests. We have suggested that given their inferior position in the relationship, there are often strong tendencies encouraging workers to mobilise collectively to have any chance of counter-balancing employer power. This tendency is not uniform amongst all workers and hindered, as we noted, by various counter-pressures and difficulties. In recent times newer types of employment relations actors have emerged on the stage, usually to support workers who are denied or do not have access to union representation.[20] Finally comes the state. Much like the headmaster in *if....* or the civil servant mandarin in *Yes Minister*, state agencies may have their own independent agendas but also seek to secure stability, order and legitimacy. For structural reasons the state is likely to have one eye on maintaining favourable conditions for business investment, while at the same time being sensitive to the need to maintain industrial peace and wider social consent. The manner in which the state 'balances' these competing interests will depend on a variety of different factors including economic conditions, objectives for welfare support, pressures from global businesses, labour mobilisation and union strength, and the political preferences of a ruling party. Having now considered some of the key actors involved in regulating the employment relationship, our next two chapters will look at how they interact in terms of the processes of ER. First we will examine ER processes of cooperation, followed by consideration of conflict and strike processes.

5

Collaboration and Consent: Cooperation at Work

introduction

While The Beatles are widely recognised as Liverpool's second greatest musical export after the band The Farm, they are perhaps less known for their analysis of bargaining, negotiation and cooperation. Yet The Beatles' song 'We Can Work It Out' offers an account of negotiations that many a seasoned bargainer in employment relations could easily relate to. The song charts the ups and downs of a negotiation between two equally hardnosed and, ultimately, constructive protagonists. Struggling to hammer out an agreement, one of the exasperated negotiators appeals: 'Try to see it my way, do I have to keep on talking till I can't go on?' He cajoles his rival by acknowledging their position, but cautions that holding out for more will simply lead negotiations to breaking point: 'while you see it your way', this negotiator warns, 'there's a chance that we may fall apart before too long!' Yet his rival remains unmoved by the entreaty and she responds with a call for sense. 'Think of what you're saying, you can get it wrong and still think that it's alright.' Similarly frustrated at the intransigence of the situation, she too offers the promise of settlement, whilst making her rival all too aware of the failure to agree: 'we can work it out and get it straight, or say good night'. Yet her opposite number, seemingly well aware of this threat, seeks to placate and appeals for conciliation: 'life is very short, and there's no time, for fussing and fighting, my friend...so I will ask you once again, try to see it my way'. The climate is clearly charged, but both parties remain optimistic, together insisting 'we can work it out'.

The dynamic of 'We Can Work It Out' is not too dissimilar to the cut and thrust of negotiations in employment relations and the subtleties involved in actively trying to ensure cooperation. In this case, we have the employer and the employee, both approaching the relationship on their own terms and from their own vantage point, and each holding different sets of interests which are invariably prone to clash. Nonetheless, just as Paul McCartney and John Lennon sang in their 1965 chart hit, the parties inevitably come to cooperate despite their differences: they 'work it out', albeit in ways very dependent on circumstance. Yet for all the attention employment relations 'fussing and fighting' attracts, interactions at work are more typically based on different varieties of cooperation.

Now this does not mean, as unitarism might assume, that employer–employee cooperation is to be naturally expected and that conflict, when it arises, is an abnormality from an otherwise consensual relationship. Cooperation has to be 'worked at' and 'worked out'. But this is not simply a matter of implementing the latest in a long line of prescriptive so-called 'best practices'. 'Working out' the strains in the relationship is made rather tricky by the concept referred to in previous chapters, 'structural antagonism' inherent in employment situations. At one level, all human labour is by definition social and cooperative. Unlike Margaret Thatcher's adage that there is no such thing as society, human labour inevitably brings together communities of people to act for some end, whether it be our neolithic ancestors colluding to hunt or our modern architects and engineers who design nuclear power plants. Indeed, even the individual and highly mobile entrepreneur, working with nothing but a smartphone, requires the social labour of possibly hundreds of Chinese workers in Shenzen to deliver that device in the first instance, not to mention all of the other human interventions in subsequently getting that phone to the entrepreneur. However, cooperative work under capitalism, as we have seen in Chapter 4, is marked by underlying tensions between the employer and the worker. The private ownership of capital brings together those whose interest is gainful accumulation of profit, which is to be generated through the effective utilisation of labour effort (the employer), and those who seek to maximise the financial reward on that labour, with some restraints on the terms upon which such labour is used (the worker). These different concerns over reward and effort have significant ramifications for whether employment relations are 'worked out' or whether things 'fall apart before too long'. It is to some of these issues that we will now turn.

cooperation through coercion

The next time you have the opportunity to visit a retail park or town centre, take a trip into a Sports Direct store. If you can avoid directing your gaze towards the Adidas Samba trainers, take a moment to observe the shop employees who work there, standing behind tills, filling racks, encouraging customers to purchase accessories, responding to radio instructions from supervisors and managers who remain hidden from view to the customers' (and workers') eyes. What you see results, in part, from the efforts of Sports Direct owner, Mike Ashley, to control and organise not only what work staff do but, importantly, how they do it. The extent to which workers do what Mike wants depends partly on the attitudes and behaviour of his staff. Perhaps irked by being called in at short notice on a zero-hour contract, staff work indifferently, adjure from 'emotional labour' and do the bare minimum to get through their shift. Or perhaps workers respond to Mike's organisation of work through enthusiastic commitment and love of the job. In both cases, employees cooperate with Mike's regime, but do so in different ways. For Mike, it is entirely possible that the former response of indifference and 'I don't care type of attitude' may be sufficient, for he may have set his expectations and job requirements so low that only a minimum level of 'compliance' with his rules and orders is required. In contrast to how the purveyors of 'employee engagement' see the world, plain compliance may suffice to meet Mike's needs; to seek anything beyond this may be unnecessary or undesirable. Certainly the media exposé about working life in Sports Direct suggests that the company, in subjecting its workers to allegedly punitive conditions of employment, has little interest in generating a 'high-commitment workplace'. Similar employment conditions like those alleged at Sports Direct have been noted elsewhere, such as the intensification of effort for both shop-floor workers and middle managers at Amazon, an organisation that actually gives its staff a distinct identity, the 'Amazonians' (Kantor and Streitfeld, 2015). Strangely, 'engagement' enthusiasts often overlook that the conditions of work which make a worker discontented and unhappy can still be economically productive for the employer (whilst conversely, workers can report job satisfaction without expressing high levels of commitment to their company or employer).

Yet for other employers, the indifferent attitude of unenthusiastic compliance may be an unattractive proposition, particularly where the job requires high levels of discretion, diligence or creativity in application. The employer, in order to hang on to such workers, may be required to offer highly attractive conditions of work to secure more than the sort of compliance that turns a profit for Mike Ashley. For these employers, the expectations and requirements for cooperation might be more ambitious, with time and effort devoted to cultivating employee motivation and commitment.

Between these opposites of compliance and commitment stand a range of possibilities which typically depend on multiple influences, like the concerns of the parties, the circumstances of local labour market, the pressures of the product market and the characteristics of the job. At one level cooperation in employment relations might be said, perhaps counterintuitively, to develop through 'coercion' (Fox, 1985). By coercion is meant the exercise of power to curb an individual's autonomy to freely choose. You might of course wonder at how cooperation, of any form, could be generated through such means. Yet for radical accounts of employment relations, the employer–worker relationship is fundamentally grounded in coercive relations and arises in a context of power and dependence. You might recall from Chapter 4 that our Rockefeller controls the resources which Kunz requires for a livelihood. This offered our employer considerable social power for his ability to control access to a livelihood is a measure of the worker's dependence. While Mr Kunz might well be theoretically free to work for someone else or opt out of employment relations by setting up his own business or become a New Age traveller, the entire class of workers, of which Kunz is representative, cannot have that option. Workers are, as Gerald Cohen (1983) the political philosopher put it, 'collectively unfree' given their reliance on capitalists to earn their crust. This relationship of power and dependence is often visibly illustrated in the threat of 'the sack' and unemployment. Such a threat provides workers with a very expedient reason to offer up cooperation to avoid ending up 'on the scrapheap'.[21] Indeed the efficacy of the threat of the sack is such that should unemployment ever be eradicated from our society, employers' power and their ability to induce workforce cooperation through coercion would be seriously impeded. For example, in his seminal critique of the Keynesian policy of full employment, the economist Michael Kalecki (1943: 335) argued that:

> the maintenance of full employment would cause social and political changes which would give new impetus to the opposition of the business leaders. Under a regime of permanent full employment, 'the sack' would cease to play its role as a disciplinary measure… Business leaders class instinct tells them that lasting full employment is unsound from their point of view and that unemployment is an integral part of the normal capitalist system.

Under conditions of a tight labour market, Kalecki maintained, employers would compete with each other to hire labour. With job opportunities available elsewhere, workers' confidence to challenge the terms on which they offered their cooperation would increase vis-à-vis their employers. The rather provocative conclusion is that unemployment, or at least increasing the precariousness of stable and regular employment, is good for capitalists. We might not be so surprised then that on observing the impact of mass unemployment in the 1980s, the then head of the Treasury Sir Douglas Wass could opine:

> [That] what has emerged in shop-floor behaviour through fear and anxiety is much greater than I think could have been done by more co-operative methods...There is a potential for productivity growth on a scale we have not had in this country. (Cited in Riddell, 1983: 78)

Yet inducing worker compliance through raising the precariousness of employment can, in some countries at least, be even more extreme. As Qatar prepares for the 2022 World Cup, construction firms' 'global talent management strategies' involve sourcing Nepalese and Bangladeshi migrant labour to build the new stadia. Yet several reports indicate that workers are forced to surrender to employers their passports upon arrival in the country, restricting freedom of movement. Housed in crude accommodation and forced to work in conditions of extreme heat with little access to water, many workers are reported to have died from cardiac arrest on construction sites. Yet workers are hesitant to protest, for they face the prospect of deportation by the authorities; in one case, over 100 striking workers who refused to cooperate with their employer were expelled from the country in 2015. It is a sad measure of the desperation of many sections of the global pool of human talent that there are those who would rather risk death building football stadiums than return to their homelands, where prospects are deemed even bleaker.[22]

At this point we should note that blatant coercion to induce cooperation has its limits. Those who exercise it must tread carefully. Even in the brutalised environment of a forced labour camp, the authorities would engage in positive cajolement with prisoners to safeguard the basic cooperation needed to fulfil work duties (as recounted in Alexsandr Solzhenitsyn's 1962 semi-autobiographical account, *One Day in the Life of Ivan Denisovich*). If this is true of the work camp, then it is certainly true of the modern employment relationship. A scenario whereby the powerful rely exclusively on coercion to induce cooperation is likely to have its limits, resulting, at best, in passive indifference, at worse, militant resistance and strikes (more on these in Chapter 6). For those aware that their employers are using their position of power to impose terms and conditions of employment will likely mobilise what power resources they can muster in return to seek a change in the arrangement. Power and dependence work both ways. Workers, albeit to a lesser degree, also retain an ability to coerce the other side to agree or concede to conditions more favourable to their interests. This might be achieved through combining in trade unions, engaging in indifferent and unproductive labour, obstructiveness or sabotage, high turnover or absence. In these situations, cooperation is likely to be 'worked out' through a power struggle as each side seeks to impose their favoured terms of cooperation upon the other. Tom Juravich's (1988) *Chaos on the Shop Floor*, an ethnographic account of adversarial employment relations at a small American manufacturer, provides an exemplar of just such a workplace, as indeed do many of the earlier episodes of *Coronation Street* involving Mike Baldwin, the uncompromising owner of the knickers factory, who would constantly threaten workers with the sack if he thought they were slacking or in any way appeared to be getting above 'their social standing'.[23]

The consequences of such struggles are nonetheless likely to be disruptive socially, politically and economically. A process of compromise that seeks to 'work it out' will likely follow. For if workers conscious of their coerced conditions can mobilise to strike back in some manner at their employers, the latter must consider whether the advantages they secure from an exchange based on the exercise of naked power outweigh its costs. In a context of intense market competition between firms, for example, adversarial relations of this sort may become unworkable. Harry Katz's (1985) account of the American auto industry, *Shifting Gears*, is instructive here. An industry traditionally marked by employer authoritarianism was threatened by wildcat militant unionism in a series of power struggles during the 1930s and 1940s. Begrudgingly employers conceded union recognition and adversarial relations became institutionalised in the periodically scheduled negotiation of a collective bargaining contract. Cooperative relations with the auto plants took a highly contractual form as each party sought to hold the other rigidly to some predetermined set of contract terms based on tight job descriptions, grievance procedures and seniority rules. However, as local markets were exposed to Japanese imports from the late 1970s onwards, this regime of institutionalised adversarial cooperation became problematic. With profit margins squeezed, Ford, General Motors and Chrysler sought to escape from the constraints of union power through a new approach. First, the 'Southern Strategy' of redirecting investment away from the heavily unionised states of Michigan, Indiana and Ohio to new plants in the non-union states of Kentucky, South Carolina and Tennessee was used. Second, employers then set out to divide and rule the collectively organised power of labour by coercing, often through veiled threats of site closure or relocation, the union plants in the North into accepting new labour relations practices which had been applied, with greater ease, in the non-union South.

The tactic is known as 'whipsawing' employment relations. The new practices were often inspired by Japanese management philosophies and sought to move away from traditions of workplace adversarialism which the 'Big Three' US car manufacturers attributed to the coercive gamesmanship of the collective bargaining contract. Attempts to foster more willing cooperation from the workforce were pursued in new forms of 'teamwork' and team leaders, 'quality circles' and other HRM techniques which tended to involve the dilution of formerly tightly specified bargaining contracts.

Although reliance on coercion and power pressure tactics remains for many employers as a viable strategy, others have felt they should moderate such methods and search for alternative ways to promote compliance. In practice, employers often use a judicious blend of coercion and consent; even in the auto industry examples above, practices designed to enhance commitment co-existed with the blunt stick of 'whipsawing'. But generally, most sophisticated managers prefer to rule by consent. The same is largely true of employees. Workers can and do seek to impose their preferred mode of cooperation on employers; think of the institutional arrangement of the 'closed shop', for example, where unionised workers could dictate the terms upon which a worker could be hired (although in some cases this arrangement could also suit the employer). To a much rarer degree, workers who are highly skilled, sought after and difficult to replace can also impose their own terms of hire upon the employer: the former Arsenal striker Gervinho demanded a helicopter and a private beach when he negotiated a contract with a United Arab Emirates club, for example (although even the club eventually balked at the demands and walked away).[24] But for most workers, such strategies are either impossible or hazardous to pursue. In most cases, workers need to undertake or threaten independent, collective mobilisation backed up by costly strike action for such pressure tactics to work. As the chapter on 'Conflict' will demonstrate next, this is not easy or very palatable for many workers. Of course there remain some, like those workers organised in the traditionally communist French Confédération Générale du Travail (CGT), who will prefer to opt for a militant power struggle in their dealings with employers, but these remain a minority. More likely is that workers seek to cooperate on more consensual terms of exchange, perhaps exemplified by the institutionalisation of consent that underpins the social partnership approach preferred by, for example, the Finnish SAK, the Central Organisation of Finnish Trade Unions. So it is to a consideration of these types of cooperation we now turn.

cooperation through consent

Most political leaders, in justifying a contentious new policy, are prone to talk in terms of the 'national interest'. This involves an appeal to the people of a particular territory, assumed to be united by history, language or culture, to subordinate whatever sectional interests they individually hold, for the good of the country. The image our leaders will conjure is one where all members of the community share a common objective and should, for the benefit of this shared purpose, willingly accept their leaders' direction and cooperate with full commitment. Such appeals are common in times of political or economic crisis, especially in times of war, and are effective in binding otherwise divided sections of the population together. Given the potency of such appeals in the political sphere, it is no surprise that similar exhortations are common among 'captains of industry'. There is the longstanding asinine unitarist ideology we discussed in Chapter 2 that prevails amongst employers, envisaging everyone in the company cooperating harmoniously in pursuit of shared interests and where the employers' leadership is unquestionably accepted. The small family firm of the owner–manager and the associated informal and friendly relations that characterise this environment are sometimes idealised as archetypal of unitary cooperation. In reality, however, membership of such putative communities is more typically a product of calculative expedience around the need for profit and wages than the feelings associated with, say, 'love of country' or 'family harmony in a corporation'. Cooperation in employment relations, as we observed earlier, cannot be simply appealed for; it has to be 'worked out'.

Attempts to imbue cooperation between employer and employee with a more developed sense of fidelity have nevertheless a long history (for an account of this see Rose, 1978). Often the efforts are employer led and are targeted to appeal to some combination of either the pecuniary impulses of the worker or their alleged social needs for more involvement and wellbeing in work. The former appeal by employers for cooperation has taken different forms. At its weakest, it amounts to an employer encouraging workers to consent, on an open-ended basis, for management know best how to run the company and a successful enterprise will maintain jobs, wages and be good for workers. This appeal is actually weak because there is no guarantee a profitable and successful firm will continue to provide for workers' needs on any ongoing basis. Indeed owners, such as our Rockefeller, may decide to redirect their excess cash into a new line of profit-making that is external to the firm and, in the process, leave Mr Kunz on another scrapheap.

As we discussed in Chapter 3, there are forces from financialisation that affect employment security and wellbeing, with companies seeking a profitable return not via the effort of labour but from purchasing and then simply 'asset stripping' a going concern. In such highly unpredictable and volatile employer–employee relationships, appeals for cooperation are also unconvincing insofar as they rely on the expectation that workers should cooperate by simply taking on trust that in the unspecified future management will allocate unspecified rewards which will meet workers' aspirations. Imagine a *Dragons' Den* investor being asked to donate their money on the basis of vague appeals to emotional loyalty, identity and pride in a product with unspecified returns; one can imagine the outcome. Unsurprising then that vague employer appeals of this sort regularly fall flat with most workers.

You might think that formal schemes of profit-share overcome this problem. A pivotal element of such schemes is that they are intended to raise worker motivation that leads to greater cooperation, insofar as they entitle them to a share of the company profits they make: 'the harder we all work for the company, the more we shall all share', an employer is likely to propose to the workforce, perhaps even specifying an expected or anticipated percentage payout in the future, if all goes to plan. But even here the basis on which such schemes are held to generate stronger forms of cooperation can be questioned. The determination of a company's profits are likely to depend upon a great many influences that destabilise even the best laid plans: consumer demand for the product, the nature of competition in the product market, fluctuations in interest rates on loanable funds, oscillations in international exchange rates which might harm trade in export markets and so on. Additional outlays in worker productivity are but one factor impacting upon profits and, it should be said, probably an uncertain one given the breadth of additional influences. No matter how impressed the worker might be with the employers' clarion call to share in profits, if there is, inter alia, no consumer demand for the product, the additional exertions of labour effort will come to nought. Indeed, it is all the more plausible that the intelligent worker, embarking on the daily shift, will rationalise that the likely contribution of their individual effort in determining the share of profits will be negligible (or at least they can free ride) given the host of other factors lying beyond their control and often beyond the influence of their immediate manager or supervisor too. This is not to say profit-sharing is ineffective. Much depends perhaps on the institutional design of such schemes. For example, an interesting form of 'profit-sharing' is the one proposed by the German Confederation of Trade Unions (DGB) in the 1980s: instead of higher wages cutting into profits and leading to inflationary price increases or disinvestment and unemployment, a tax on profits could be skimmed into a collective fund controlled by the unions to be used as capital for socially desirable investment. A similar concept was mooted by the Swedish LO union confederation under the 'Worker Fund' scheme. An equally novel experiment has been the Mondragon federation of worker-owned cooperatives in the Basque country, while in the UK the John Lewis Partnership (department stores and supermarkets) is probably the best-known employee-owned company, where each employee has the potential to influence the business through branch forums and divisional councils. Workers receive a share of the profits, which is typically a substantial contributor to their salary.

More popular than profit-share amongst contemporary human resource managers, however, appears to be some variant of incentive-based or variable payment system. Employers often like such schemes as they seem to provide a straightforward motivational technique which limits the costs of workforce monitoring and supervision. Yet while incentive pay schemes are designed to elicit cooperation through rewarding the hardworking over the idle, such methods have been frequently confounded by employee experience that they divide and weaken the workforce. Rather than engender cooperation, incentive schemes regularly fermented restrictive practices and informal control of output in the manufacturing industries where they were traditionally widespread – a form of inter-worker cooperation or 'systematic soldiering' that was of little added value to the employer. Recent experiments in 'performance related pay' similarly point to a paradoxical outcome in enlisting worker cooperation. Where targets are unattainable, assessments are contaminated by managerial bias or scores are manipulated into the forced distributions of artificial 'bell-curves'; increased jealousies and decreased morale follow suit. So-called individualised incentives potentially undermine cooperative team-working efforts. There is probably a lesson here for those of you who may be budding human resource managers once you graduate: whilst financial rewards are generally the motivation for workers entering into an employment relationship, they also have an interest in things like fairness and justice. Where these are sorely lacking, the carrot of financial return may be subject to diminishing returns. In any case, the paradoxical consequences of performance related pay might lead one to suspect that employers use these techniques, not so much to foster cooperation or motivate workers into more effort but to transfer an element of risk for the lack of business success to the worker or to encourage an individual as opposed to collective response to problems at work.

Aside from remuneration packages, employers have also sought to enlist higher levels of cooperation through meeting the social needs or wellbeing of workers. The motives, practices and consequences of such offerings are as diverse as they are complex, varying widely from work–life balance arrangements to 'Hawaiian Shirt Days' (mocked to great effect in the film *Office Space*). Some of the practices adopted have been substantive and relatively progressive, like the model villages of New Lanark or Port Sunlight where the local employer provided housing, child care and education at a time when the state was unwilling to do so. More contemporaneously, Apple now offer to freeze the ova of female employees based in the United States. *The Guardian* (2015) reported Apple claiming that it:

> cares deeply about employees and their families, and we are always looking at new ways our health programmes can meet their needs. We continue to expand our benefits for women, with a new extended maternity leave policy, along with cyropreservation and egg storage as part of our extensive support for infertility treatments…We want to empower women at Apple to do the best work of their lives as they care for loved ones and raise their families.[25]

Google have designed their engineering headquarters in Switzerland with meeting 'pods' in the style of igloos, fireman poles to allow easy access between floors, a chill-out aquarium and a slide to ensure that people can get to the cafeteria as quickly as possible. 'The lava lamps, free food and games are all part of the Google culture…it is informal and a structure that isn't dictated from the top', the vice president of Google Engineering earnestly claimed.[26] That the provision of trinkets and office furnishings is thought sufficient to generate the 'right' kind of employee commitment amongst adults might, of course, seem like the worst kind of paternalist condescension, reflected in Exhibit Box 5.1. Thus it is not too surprising that many workers view faddish employer ideas to engender labour commitment – such as 'informal casual Fridays' or 'Hawaiian Shirt Days' – as trivial window dressing, attempts to distract from schemes that intensify work or at best provide temporary relief from the monotony of low discretion job tasks.

Nevertheless, some employers have moved beyond igloos and aquariums to provide more consequential ways to secure worker cooperation. As we will discuss further in Chapter 7, a great deal of attention and research has been directed towards giving employees a voice, in the hope they are then better committed and engaged. The logic of such initiatives stems from the belief that people are likely to respond positively to decisions they have been involved in or influenced. One of the surest ways this might be achieved in an economy is through workplace democratisation, co-determination and joint regulation. However, as

Exhibit Box 5.1   A manager, observing his employees at work, begins to doubt the morale boosting effects of the company's new 'Dress Down Friday' initiative.

Credit: Ronald Grant Archive

Chapter 7 will discuss, when asked to consider genuine worker empowerment and participation as a way to work out the strains in the employment relationship, managers are more likely to turn their attention to a plethora of employer-controlled schemes like job enrichment, quality circles, team briefings or staff consultative forums. While there is a great deal of dissimilarity across these techniques, they at least all share the common motive of being efforts to ensure greater receptivity and enthusiasm for employer objectives at work. Such efforts, whilst often desirable from the employees' immediate point of view and in some cases a spur to encouraging richer cooperative efforts on their part, do have their problems. For a start, time and time again, involvement and participatory efforts are constructed to address issues presumed by employers to be of equal concern to manager and worker alike, with a low tolerance for divisive or conflictual matters which might independently concern the employee. Here and there workers might be empowered to make some decisions under the sponsorship of a quality circle or a consultative forum, but only if they deal with, for employers at least, the right issues. Inconvenient choices are soon marginalised or fall on deaf ears. Instead of genuine co-determination, various in-house involvement and participation schemes end up as downward communication, explaining why a management decision took the form it did. They are not designed so that workers might press employers into *committing* to particular policy. That would entail, for employers at least, an uninvited exercise of power.

In light of such experiences worker aspirations are stonewalled and left unfulfilled as the expected quid pro quo for greater effort on their part rarely amounts to much of substance. If not cynically derided, employee participation becomes seen by those subjected to it as little more than work intensification. As a worker in one celebrated study reflected on a job-involvement scheme, 'I never feel enriched, I just feel knackered' (Nichols and Beynon, 1977: 253). While greeted with initial waves of enthusiasm, time sees involvement and participation schemes fall by the wayside because workers learn of their limits, employer attention is turned elsewhere or their expectations for transformative levels of worker cooperation fail to bear fruit and so their appeal wanes. The key lesson here is that employer concerns are not in the final instance directed to meeting workers' wellbeing but to ensuring profitable accumulation of wealth for business owners. Packages ostensibly designed to meet workers' social needs tend to function on this basis in many instances. When firms are subject to significant downturns in profits, the stark cash nexus of the employment relationship reasserts itself and a concern with meeting the workers' 'wellbeing' must inevitably get cast to the four winds whatever the honest intentions of the employer might be. A good example here is the Volvo experiments at Kalmar and Uddevalla in Sweden (Berggren, 1992). Faced with problems of labour turnover, Volvo management embraced new ideas around job enrichment, rotation and enlargement, and even moved away from assembly line operations to stationary production. Despite occurring with union involvement and support, and delivering substantial gains to workers, the company disbanded the experiments when it no longer became profitable to sustain them. The point here is that the need for ongoing profit-making places strict limits on what employer-led efforts to enlist active cooperation can achieve. The tempest of a financially impelled capitalism prevents employers, in the words of Paul Thompson (2003), from 'keeping their side of the bargain'.

Workers who are exposed to strategies to engender consent and cooperation may come to see themselves as the victim of a cruel confidence trick, like the prisoners in Plato's parable of the cave. Rather than being a 'talent' to be 'engaged', they are now just a number in a 'headcount' whose fate is determined by the pecuniary 'bottom line'. Attempts by the employer to later rehabilitate themselves in the eyes of workers and repair the broken strains of the employment relationship may be greeted with a seedbed of cynicism and mistrust rather than any further offer of enthusiastic cooperation. As The Beatles warn, goodwill and harmony can break down between the two parties and, before too long, the relationship can 'fall apart'. On this image one is reminded of the video going around social media showing a room full of workers at a Carrier air conditioning plant in the United States being told by a company executive that the factory is being moved to Mexico and that they're all going to lose their jobs. Asking people to lower their murmurs so that he can 'share' his 'information', the Carrier executive justifies the need to 'stay competitive' and 'the extremely price-sensitive marketplace'. Conceding the difficult news, he then asks employees to continue to cooperate in manufacturing the 'same high quality product' during the shutdown. 'F**k you!' a worker shouts back.[27]

There are of course many good employers and there do exist many happy workers doing productive and fulfilling work. Employer attempts to enlist cooperation and consent can work. As employees we all know the difference between good and bad employers and good and bad management. While there are pressures on employers there remains scope for better or worse management. For example, in the USA, the New England grocery chain Market Basket fired its long-time CEO despite him being seen as looking after employees and customers when the company emphasised the need for greater shareholder return. However, a range of employees – other executives, store managers, cashiers, drivers and warehouse workers – all protested with rallies to allow the CEO to return. Further, customers boycotted stores and pledged support on social media networks. Although there was no union, employees still demonstrated important agency mobilisation by banding together to preserve the company's image and counter a perceived employment relations injustice.

In any case, most of us would rather slither down a fireman's pole at Google than be subject to the claimed daily searches at Sports Direct, allegedly involving workers stripped to the final layer above the waist as part of the store's zero tolerance theft policy. What Sundar Pichai, the CEO of Google, provides to his workforce appears infinitely more desirable than what Mike Ashley demands of his workers. It is true that many employers have the wherewithal, motive and means to make cooperative initiatives work. Despite the possible gains from cooperation, too many employers either bypass or dismiss such schemes as they do not see them serving their immediate interests. Consequently, alternative ways to structure cooperation at work that are independent of unchecked employer preferences are important to study. This brings us to consideration of the law and collective bargaining to support cooperation.

cooperation through bargaining and the law

The legal requirement for profit sharing in France, provision for works councils in Germany or statutory support for union recognition in Britain, Canada and even the USA all testify to the centrality of the law in structuring how employers and employees cooperate at work. Now, in some quarters, the law is seen as providing 'excessive' rights for workers and imposing 'burdensome' obligations on employers, but in reality law structures the employment relationship in ways that can favour *either* party. So the UK Health and Safety at Work Act 1974 provides a framework of rights wherein employers cannot simply expect workers to cooperate in a setting that is harmful to their welfare. For some UK construction firms this law is often viewed as regulatory 'red tape' and they have been quite keen to 'blacklist' workers who seek to enforce it. On the other hand, the UK Trade Union Act 2016, requiring unions to cooperate with employers before undertaking industrial strikes by providing notice of ballots and subsequent action, would seem to be a form of unnecessary 'red tape', yet it curries favour with many (but not all) employers as it tries to eliminate wildcat action and supresses workers rights to engage in strike action (more on strikes in our next chapter).

The different prospects provided by the law stem in part from the complex balancing act it plays between satisfying the need for profitable accumulation by employers on the one hand and the need for social legitimacy on the other, by ensuring workers are protected from the worst excesses of employer power. How well the law achieves this depends partly on circumstances, namely the political balance of power between employer and employee, and also on a general requirement to support the conditions for private business to flourish. For example, should the balance of political power swing too firmly in the direction of workers, resulting in a raft of pro-labour legislation, concerns may be expressed that business investment would soon take flight. Yet push too far the other way and expose workers too harshly to the diktats of the market, and government lawmakers may face defeat at the polling booth come the next election.

In the earliest phases of industrialisation, the law, wholly subservient to the employer class, was wielded to guarantee a supply of acquiescent labour by prohibiting many attempts by workers to bend the terms of cooperation in their favour. But consistent with what we have said about coercive employer attempts to ensure cooperation and compliance, this strategy proved, in the long run, unstable. Through a mixture of elite sensitivity to the demands of the working classes and the capacity of the latter to push through reforms in their favour, the terms upon which cooperative labour would be supplied changed in various countries through Factory Acts and Labour Codes. These struggles are not confined to the history books and continue today in the street demonstrations over the 2016 El Khomri labour reforms in France or the 2011 Wisconsin Act 10 protests over public sector bargaining rights in the US. This delicate balancing act between profitable accumulation and social legitimacy is also exemplified by the history of the European Union. On the one hand, the European project, represented by the Single European Act 1986, is organised to provide a continental-wide market for business as well creating new opportunities for private profit, by breaking up state monopolies. Yet the longstanding social democratic view within the European project, epitomised by the likes of Jacques Delors, has been wary about the move to a single free market, fearing that the move to free competition across the continent risked a race to the bottom and social dumping. Alongside the economic market has traditionally been the desire for a complementary social model to promote better equality and harmonisation between member states. Thus the Social Chapter ensured legitimacy for the European project by promoting employment rights through the creation of legal structures that enforced minimum standards of safety, working hours, contractual rights and worker participation across Europe. TUPE, that is the Transfer of Undertakings (Protection of Employment) Regulations 2006 (and not Donald Trump's hair) is an exemplar of how the European Union has sought to combine the market and the social: providing contractual protection and consultation rights to workers in the situation of mergers and acquisitions.

Whilst the law can be infinitely superior to reliance on the paternalistic predilections of the employer for ensuring that workers have a right to 'work out' the terms upon which they cooperate, it is often insufficient in reaching into the everyday cut and thrust of the employment relationship. In many cases it offers little else than a 'floor of rights' upon which cooperation might proceed. As such, the law is often remote. Few ER actors know their rights and obligations, and many employers have the means and motive to avoid them in ways to disadvantage workers. Most individual employees often lack not just knowledge but the time, resources and determination to ensure their rights are upheld. If workers are to have a degree of self-management and control over the terms upon which collaboration is offered, the law then is clearly lacking. As was shown for our Mr Kunz in Chapter 4, some resolution to such lack of power and self-determination lies in the alternative of collective bargaining and negotiation.

The relevance of collective bargaining lies in accepting that divergent interests and concerns need to be 'worked out', employers and employees should *negotiate* the terms on which cooperation is to be provided. Negotiations involve not just the art of persuasion and force of argument but the effective threat of power and sanction. The negotiators' attempts at 'attitudinal structuring' found in 'We Can Work It Out', for example, were only meaningful if the threat to walk away and 'say goodnight' was sufficiently detrimental to the interests of the other party. Unsurprisingly, many employers have long been uncomfortable with negotiating with their workforces collectively, for political and economic reasons. Politically, collective bargaining potentially limits, to various degrees, the exercise of the employer's social power. Economically, where negotiations occur on matters like wages and effort, it potentially results in workers claiming a share of the firm's profit that they would otherwise not receive had they relied on employers' goodwill. Yet where collective bargaining prevails, how the conflicts of interest over issues of difference are 'worked out' will vary.

It has been commonplace when discussing collective negotiations in the instructional textbooks to refer to the opposed strategies of 'distributive bargaining' (where the goals of the parties are in fundamental conflict with each other but where zero-sum deals have to be struck to ensure ongoing cooperation) and 'integrative bargaining' (where the parties focus on shared problems and attempt to secure mutually beneficial outcomes). Whilst a useful way to think about different types of negotiations, in reality what often pass for integrative outcomes in employment relations are simply calculated attempts at chicanery and incorporation. Even apparently integrative gains have ultimately to be distributed. This aside, the skill and expertise of the negotiators and their backing amongst their constituents will surely count, but so do other issues beyond their control, such as state of play in the product or labour market. Crucial too, from an ER perspective is the role of institutions and the level at which bargaining occurs. Take, for example, the German system of ER. Often noted for its cooperative aspects, Germany has historically been marked by sector-level collective bargaining. Yet bitter conflict, strike action and lockouts have been known to presage agreements at this level. However, once the divisive detail at sectoral level has been 'worked out', the employers and workers at plant level can focus, through the institution of works councils, on the more consensual and cooperative elements of work and employment.

In any event, as we saw in Chapter 3, prospects for collective bargaining are being marginalised as employer unilateralism over the terms and conditions of employment increasingly holds sway. Even where formal bargaining processes remain they are progressively hollowed out, becoming little else than empty shells and one-sided cooperation as employees are impelled to offer up 'concessions' under the threat of job loss. Recent decades have seen employers narrowing the range of issues over which bargaining takes place, or edging the process to one of 'consultation' rather than negotiation, or to one of just 'information provision' rather than consultation. The general erosion of collective bargaining, particularly in Anglo-Saxon countries, has led to some soul searching about how to increase trade union relevance. In countries like Australia, the UK, the US and Ireland, one strand of thought has been that a future for collective bargaining might be secured if unions can find some way to sell it to employers. That is, unions and collective bargaining need to be packaged as a sort of cooperative adjunct to the employer's quest for increased profit, competitiveness and effective management of change. This strategy is termed 'partnership' and in recent years has become something of a (contested) fashion in labour and union circles. It relies on promoting cooperative rather than adversarial employment relations with management, on the assumption that it will strengthen union presence in the workplace and deliver some form of mutual gain. Having workplace presence, it is maintained, ipso facto, provides protection for workers and might even help grow union membership. This debate on partnership in the academic literature is generally fascinating. At one end, those whom we might call 'the critics' have marshalled evidence to suggest that partnership strategies offer up worker cooperation on terms that are all too favourable for employers, with little reciprocity for workers (and union members) in return (Kelly, 2004). Under this interpretation, unions risk becoming the industrial equivalent of Beecher Stowe's 'Uncle Tom' on the slave plantation: appeasing authority and complicit in the oppression of their own people. For the critics, workers and their unions would be better served through an emphasis on contesting, not cooperating with, employer dominance at work. Yet those, whom we might call the 'optimists' on partnership, suggest that it is better to be a collaborationist than not to exist at all (Johnstone and Wilkinson, 2016). What's more, they argue, real gains for workers ensue through a more cooperative approach (Rubinstein and Kochan, 2001). Arbitrating between these competing perspectives is no easy task. Both approaches tend to slide into an either/or posture that one approach is superior to the other. Yet while partnership may work at different points in time and space, in a context of uncertain profit-making, where the employment relationship is being continuously organised and with only temporary compromises the result, there surely remain many ways for unions to skin a cat.

▬▬▬ conclusion

We have seen in this chapter that cooperation is a multi-layered and complex phenomenon in employment relations. From the induced compliance of coercion to the sophisticated cultivating of consent, cooperation takes many forms, dependent on the vicissitudes of circumstance. Too often, however, the base upon which contemporary workplace cooperation proceeds is shaped and dictated to by the employer, whether evident in the crass rules and edicts of Sports Direct and Amazon or the polished manipulations of Google. Yet if there is one thing that we might take from our recourse to The Beatles, perhaps it is this: rather than one voice prevailing above all others, as is increasingly the case in modern formulations of workplace cooperation, differences of interest are best 'worked out' through an open and forthright dialogue as captured in the exchange sung by Paul and John. If our political leaders' frequent championing of pluralist democracy is to be nothing else than a pretence then each side in the employment relationship should be free to raise their voice, express their perspective and marshal their power in a context where both parties are committed to finding a jointly 'worked out' and negotiated compromise. Yet even the most well-intentioned negotiations fall down with consequential disagreement and even strike action. Conflict is as central to ER as is cooperation. On that basis we turn to a consideration of conflict in our next chapter.

6

Strikes and Strife: Conflict at Work

■■■■■■ introduction

Imagine the scene of a modern corporate boardroom. The executive directors are assembled. News is not good: company profits are down for the third year in succession. Competitors from abroad are swamping the market with cheaper, higher-quality products. The company order book gathers dust while the plant warehouse swells with unsold goods. Shareholders are edgy, threatening to disinvest should dividends not improve. The financial media have put the spotlight on a collective agreement recently signed between management and the union and claim it now looks a bad deal for the plant. Shareholders agree and start to wonder, 'Why should workers get a rise?' when they may lose dividends. Profligate allowances and lavish pension contributions, they murmur, mean that flexibility is non-existent. Company directors agree too, and if profits are to be saved a bold cost-cutting strategy will need to be implemented. A spate of layoffs will be necessary with potentially more to follow, future investment in plant halted and a project team assembled to assess cheaper production locations abroad. Directors feel the media must be informed to reassure 'the markets'. Employees must know the consequences of not meeting the challenges ahead!

Headlines roll across the airwaves that evening: 'Layoffs expected at plant!' 'Company to offshore!' 'Plant closure imminent!' Employees and their families grow apprehensive. Others in the locality also feel worried; many depend on the plant as a major employer sourcing contracts for supplies with several regional firms, while the worker spending power has been a boon to the local economy. Politicians hurry to action and, on the evening news, promise to do all they can to protect jobs and safeguard investment. A local government subsidy and tax break is in the offing.

Next day, union representatives call a workforce meeting at the plant to report on their discussions with management over the concerns. 'Prospects are bleak', they inform the gathered. Management seek a two-year wage freeze; a 30 per cent reduction in pension contributions; compulsory redundancy for a third of the workforce; and reductions in job classifications to ensure greater labour mobility across the plant. 'Closure of our plant has been threatened by management', the union leaders advise. 'Production could go abroad if management's demands are not met', explains another union official. The mood amongst the assembled is sombre. Whilst a few workers suggest 'calling the management's bluff', the prevailing sentiment is that 'givebacks' must be offered to secure jobs. Concessions, severe as they may be, will be granted.

thinking about conflict

The scenario depicted above, whilst fictionalised in its specifics, reflects a general pattern that repeats itself at different times, in different places, across the world of employment relations. A similar and real-life situation where the plant closure of manufacturer Anglesy Aluminium resulted in the devastation of a local community can be studied in Dobbins et al. (2014). Employers, making what they perceive as unsatisfactory returns on investment, often target labour costs as the main set of costs they have direct influence over. Pressure will be exerted on employees to offer up efficiencies and savings to help rejuvenate profit margins. Whilst painful for those afflicted, such concessions can be necessary to ensure continuing employment. Yet you may notice that this is a chapter specifically devoted to employment relations conflict so the opening account of company restructuring may seem amiss. A standard instructional text on employment conflict will typically concern itself with matters like organised and collective industrial action: strikes, strike trends, go-slows, overtime bans and work-to-rules. Some treatments may extend into the realm of 'unorganised', individual conflict like sabotage or theft. You will notice that the emphasis in instructional texts is invariably on worker-initiated forms of conflict. True, some texts might acknowledge employer-initiated conflict in the form of union busting or lockouts, but even here the focus remains on the most blatantly conspicuous types of workplace skirmish.

The image conjured is of employment conflict akin to an Ultimate Fighting Championship spectacle: two protagonists slugging it out and trading blows until the laurel wreath of victory is secured. Such an image – often reinforced by media headlines - can *skew* students' understanding about workplace conflict in a way that often shields the powerful and their actions in society from closer scrutiny. The instructional textbooks serve us well in providing a social science description of such phenomena and trends, but they can fail to challenge assumptions many people hold about worker-led conflict and its impact. In this chapter, we shall consider the activity in a broader terrain of exchange between employer and employee, including what should be realised as employer-led (investment or corporate) strike activities. In this regard we will return to our opening scenario later in the chapter.

workers on strike

Let us begin by considering the phenomenon of workers on strike. A strike is a temporary withdrawal of labour by workers to express a grievance or enforce a particular demand (for a classic study of strikes see Hyman, 1984). It is temporary because those involved typically intend to return to their normal activities (e.g. work) at a point in time when their grievance has been resolved or their demands met in some form. Workers may return to work to allow negotiations to commence (or resume) when seeking a settlement to the issue or grievance. The processes that stand behind the organisation of strike action are typically multifaceted and complex. Take, for example, the workplace strikes that form the backdrop to the classic film series *Robocop* and *Robocop 2*. Often crudely misinterpreted as mere 'shoot-'em-ups', the *Robocop* franchise offers a keen insight into the pressures of privatisation and automation amongst a highly demoralised workforce – the police force of Detroit. The workforce has been privatised. Its new owners, Omni Consumer Products (OCP), deliberately withhold investment for adequate policing whilst also slashing wages and pensions. Interestingly, OCP's intention is to deliberately sow the seeds of police dissent and thereby spur the workforce to take strike action. A strike, the corporation hopes, will bring chaos to the streets of Detroit, fostering public outrage towards so-called work-shy police officers and help legitimise and speed-up OCP's plan for automating the job through its recently developed fleet of high-tech robotic cops. The robots will offer 'a lifetime of on-the-street law enforcement', dramatically reducing OCP's labour costs and boosting (now privatised) shareholder dividends. Oblivious to the corporate strategy, the workers (police force) fall for the trap and strike. However, the intended disruption from the industrial action is undermined by OCP's new Robocop, who, in accordance with management directives, continues to work. In one scene, Robocop walks past a picket line, continuing to 'serve the public trust, protect the innocent and uphold the law'. Collective action is in any event short lived, not simply because of 'Robocop the Strike-Breaker' but because rank-and-file police officers are unable to sustain a disciplined withdrawal of labour. They remain highly dedicated to their 'craft' and are imbued with a strong sense of public service. As one of their number cries, 'We're not plumbers. Police officers don't strike!' Indeed, the police officers demonstrate a curious degree of solidarity with Robocop, ending their strike to come to his aid when he is under attack.

Workers on strike are one of the great spectacles of social life, a mass of organisation, conflict, division and strife, and it is no wonder that they make a great subplot to many a movie or song, from one of the earliest silent films *Strike* (1924) to *On the Waterfront* (1954), *Made in Dagenham* (2010) and *Pride* (2014) – as well as the rather woeful Bon Jovi number 'Living on a Prayer'. As the Robocop films demonstrate, strikes are part and parcel of the cut-and-thrust of management–worker relations, creating all sorts of high-stake drama. Strikes can be unpleasant affairs for those involved and affected, whilst the decision to participate, or not, is often fraught with anger and anxiety. Will the strike be effective? Will co-workers come out in support? How long will it last? At what financial and social cost? How will the employer respond? Workers can be divided over the merits of taking strike action; like the police force in Robocop, some workers see striking as what *other* workers do. Even if a strike proceeds some workers may opt to stand on the picket line while others, like Robocop, continue to work. Such occurrences are not trivial and have been known to destroy families, friendships and communities. Often the fate of a 'scab' is social ostracism; had Robocop of Detroit been Robodocker of Liverpool, he may very well have ended his working days as a rusty part at the bottom of the Mersey.

Ultimately, the process of transforming individual actors into a collective group mobilised in defiance of an employer is a supremely challenging task. Individual workers bring a variety of subjective interests into the workplace, which they often strategically trade off; some workers will accept mediocre pay for pleasant conditions of work, whereas others may seek the opposite. Organising disparate interests of this sort is difficult. Employers have less difficulty in this regard, for a positive return on the rate of profit is their singular and easily identifiable objective when entering the sphere of production (Offe and Wiesenthal (1980) offer a classic theoretical statement on this matter). Furthermore, the structural setting of work is increasingly unfavourable to the collective coalescence of individual interests. Aside from the decline of union organisation, the emergence of debt servitude amongst mortgaged households makes workers reluctant to strike, while the growth in individualised payment systems, differing shift patterns, and precarious and remote working are features of contemporary employment that stymie the shared experience of work often necessary to foster collective action.

As the American sociologist Robert Putnam (2001) has argued, many of us in developed capitalist societies are increasingly 'bowling alone', that is, we are withdrawing from engagement in group and communal activities in favour of a private life devoted to consuming Simon Cowell's 'talent' shows or taking 'selfies' on our iPhones. This individual atomisation of how we live offers a further inhospitable context for getting people to think and act collectively.

If transforming individuals' consciousness into some form of collective activity is difficult enough, there is also the important matter of employer, government and state agency responses. It is true that some employers – like the fictionalised OCP – have been known to 'manufacture' strikes to cut labour costs when product demand is low. But generally, collective industrial action has the intention to frustrate employer priorities. Strikes can undermine an employer's ability to produce output and make profits. Strikes can also weaken employers' social power, their authority to command and control workers. If strikes were mostly ineffective with little impact on employers, as many naysayers of the action contend, it would be pretty difficult to explain the longstanding trend of employers mobilising to prevent and undermine them. In the 1930s, the Ford Motor Company notoriously employed a 'Service Department', comprised of former convicts, athletes, cops and gang members, to physically assault strikers outside the factory gates (Brueggemann, 2000). Gate Gourmet, the international airline catering company, was reported in 2006 to use psychological profiling of its Dublin workforce to assess and identify which workers were likely to participate in strike action.[28] Employers might also offer inducements to either prevent or cut short a strike, and certainly such offers in themselves raise all sorts of interesting scenarios insofar as they can either strengthen or weaken the resolve of those taking, or seeking to take, industrial action: should the strikers accept or push for more? Issues of power are important here for the workforce may need to think about a whole host of factors impacting upon the effect of striking, particularly if employers have credible alternatives to withstand disruption. Consulting Colin Crouch's classic, *The Logic of Collective Action* (1982), will be a worthwhile investment for further reflection on these matters.

Aside from the employer, striking workers must all contend with the machinery of the state (government) that, historically, has been unsympathetic to industrial action. The early stages of industrial capitalism were often characterised by intense government repression, as the ruling political and judicial strata regarded strikes as subversive of the social and economic order. Certainly the worst elements of state repression were blunted in many liberal and social democracies by the early decades of the 20th century, with greater liberties and protections provided for workers to strike. However, governments of various persuasions continue to undermine industrial action through statutory means. In response to rising New York public sector strikes in the 1960s, the 'Taylor Law' was passed making work stoppages by public employees punishable by fines and jail time. In Poland today, workers are obliged to give their employer at least five days' notice before strike action can take place, with a supporting ballot and a minimum 50 per cent turnout. The 'Laval' and 'Viking' rulings from the European Court of Justice impose strict 'proportionality tests' on industrial action to ensure that strikes do not encroach on freedoms to provide goods and services, while, to varying degrees, rules around balloting and picketing are regulated across many countries to prevent 'wildcat action' and to minimise disruption to employers' businesses.

Acknowledgement of the role of the mass media must be noted in shaping public opinion about conflict. There is little doubt that privately owned news conglomerates play a key role in cultivating the parameters and content of public opinion around strike action. Given that many media outlets have a history of adversarial labour relations, such as when Rupert Murdoch's *News International* group sacked nearly 6000 striking workers who were in dispute over the company's relocation to a newly created high-tech printing facility in Wapping, London, we should not assume that editorial commentaries are disinterested voices. Through the techniques of selective editing or the privileging of particular narratives, the media play a key role in portraying strikes to the public: TV coverage of striking London Underground train drivers will likely spend as much time reporting on how the action causes 'chaos' for ordinary commuters as it will focus on the issues involved in the dispute or attempts to negotiate a settlement. It would, of course, be unreasonable to claim that all media commentary is unfavourable to striking workers, for some sympathetic and balanced voices do prevail too. Yet this should not be overplayed either. As Edward Herman and Noam Chomsky's seminal *Manufacturing Consent: The Political Economy of the Mass Media* (1988) demonstrates, the profit orientation of the 'free press' and its heavy reliance on private sector advertisers tilts the editorial balance in ways that are invariably pro-employer. One may counter that such reporting merely reflects rather than shapes 'public opinion'. This certainly introduces a chick-and-egg-style problem and it is not unreasonable to accept that dominant opinions articulated in the mass media curry favour with sections of the public and, as we have found in our own teaching, the sentiments of many a student or business school academic staff member for that matter. Out of interest, ask people you know what they think about workers going on strike (including, perhaps, college lecturers and junior doctors)? Is (or should) going on strike be a basic right? In one way the answer is yes because a huge swathe of international laws says it is a right: international treaties that have been accepted by numerous governments since the Second World War (e.g. International Labour Organisation Convention in 1948 on the right to organise and bargain collectively; the European Social Charter of 1961; the United Nations' International Covenant in 1966 on Economic, Social and Cultural Rights) all underpin the right to organise and take action democratically, legally and legitimately.

A key factor in realising 'a right to strike' is of course trade union organisation. However, for those sections of the workforce who do not enjoy trade union representation or who have perhaps borne the full brunt of private sector efficiency drives, resentments can emerge: strikers are seen as greedy insiders, featherbedding only their own jobs and maintaining excessive privileges. Whatever the basis to such perceptions their effect can be to delegitimise the 'moral case' of those who do take strike action. This is particularly true of unionised public sector workers in many developed economies. Increasingly such workers not only have to withstand the counter-arguments of their employer and media experts but also hostility stemming from an unsympathetic private sector workforce (Swenson, 1992 provides an interesting example of this in Sweden and Germany).

Given the range of forces which seem to obstruct strike action it is perhaps impressive that workers can muster the resources to engage in the activity at all. It is no surprise that workplace strikes are relatively infrequent, short affairs. In reality there are likely to be millions more days lost due to negligent and poor employer health and safety practices resulting in workplace accidents than strikes. In the UK, in 2015, around 27.4 million days were lost due to work-related illness and accidents, compared to 0.8 million days of lost production due to industrial disputes.[29] While all sorts of difficulties exist around measuring and comparing strike activity internationally, it is generally accepted that industrial strikes have registered a significant decline in OECD countries in recent decades. Aside from the challenges noted above, structural economic change has been important. If we look at the UK, the historically 'strike prone' industries were automobile manufacturing, dock work and coal mining. Today, automobile factories are increasingly automated with a relatively small workforce 'whipsawed' by the threat of capital flight to plants abroad. Dockers have been displaced by containerisation while the last UK mine shut in December 2015 as energy policy has progressively shifted to alternative sources and imports. New sectors have emerged with new types of workers unschooled and unfamiliar with long traditions of workplace organisa-tion and strike. Despite decline and the relative rarity of strikes in our time, the spectre of the striking worker continues to haunt those in power. As noted above, the UK Conservative government imposed even further legal restrictions in order to prohibit strike action and picketing. Despite a context of historic laws in preventing strikes, the 2016 Trade Union Act reopened a fractious debate on the legitimacy of strike action in public policy and civil rights debates. The defenders of the Act main-tained that strikes have consequences of the most disruptive kind to businesses, consumers and the wider public. The argument is often cast in language that appears reasonable and based on 'common sense' by having the 'interests' of either 'the public' or 'the economy' in mind, despite the fact that the interests of these two reified actors seem to regularly change depending on which political party holds office. It is true that strikes can be disruptive, are often driven by purely sectional interests and can have undesirable social, political and economic out-comes. Rather than make any assessment at this point, however, it may be useful to return to consider what a strike fundamentally represents.

thinking about strike behaviour

Strikes – whether by workers or employers – need not be seen in good or bad terms per se. The reason French airline pilots decided to embark on a strike over pay cuts when they did, during the Euro 2016 football tournament, ought to be seen as a reflection of the particular bargaining power and advantage of that group at that time. As we have seen in our prior discussion of Rockefeller and Mr Kunz in Chapter 4, workers are in the business of making a return on their investment, the investment being their labour effort which they expend in production for a finan-cial return. The capacity to labour is in many ways an attribute inherent to the individual worker and might be plausibly understood as their innate 'property' which, under contractual conditions of an employ-ment contract, they hand over to the employer for a given period of time. Indeed the capacity for labour operates like an 'investment fund' for the worker, its investment in a particular contract of employment offers financial rewards to the individual which they would otherwise not secure or, assuming they have the freedom to do so, might choose to 'invest' elsewhere. Given the variety of complex factors which can influence the conditions of ongoing labour supply and given that the buyer and seller of labour hold different interests over rewards and effort, circumstances can arise where the seller of labour becomes dis-satisfied with the terms on which their labour is being supplied. This is particularly so when we realise that the conditions under which the supply of labour operates are imbued with concerns around fairness, dignity and respect as much as interest in purely economic rewards.

If we accept the possibility for circumstances to arise wherein the supplier of labour (employee) becomes dissatisfied with the 'return' on their investment as variously defined, say the rate of pay or hours of work, then such episodes suggest that it would be unwise, even irrational, for the worker to continue to invest their effort at the same level unchecked. If of course the buyer (employer) believes the seller (worker) would never re-evaluate their supply under conditions of dissatisfactory return, then employees have little or no power of influence over their conditions, and management can proceed as before without constraint. The ability to check, curtail or withdraw the supply of labour effort is what offers workers some power in what is essentially an unequal relationship that typically favours the buyer (employer).

In Chapter 3 we discovered that the financial investor of money capital might under conditions of dissatisfaction simply switch their funds to another source. Whilst this remains plausible for employers seeking new financial returns from using their accumulated wealth and innumerable market options, it remains less true for workers who are often dependent on management for their jobs and livelihood. In theory exit options exist for workers, and high staff turnover can become a problem for employers (the buyers of labour power), but for reasons of labour mobility, employment opportunities and job search, exit is rarely a realistic or feasible route. It may therefore be more useful for the seller to try to negotiate that supply, using their labour resource as negotiating leverage over the buyer. In this way the strike (or threat of a strike) might represent one point in the spectrum of negotiation over labour supply, rather than as media reporters dramatically put it, a breakdown of negotiations. It is negotiation by other means, a temporary withdrawal of the labour resource that sits alongside other collective forms of supply regulation: work to rule, go slow, overtime ban, sit-down strike or working without enthusiasm. Each holds different degrees of impact whose relative merits for deployment must be considered on a case-by-case basis. Like any good investor, such negotiations must be engaged in shrewdly, minimising loss and maximising gain.

Whilst we might accept this analogy of why workers withdraw, one might still be tempted to argue that this hardly makes striking socially desirable. Let us consider the arguments that are used by those who would seek to deny the legitimacy of conflict. A common argument amongst employers is around 'property rights'. The crux of this argument is that strikes obstruct an employer's ability to legitimately go about their daily private business. Policy makers are often sensitive to this argument, hence the rules that exist in many countries on the picketing of employer premises and those which proscribe any obstruction of an employer's continued right to trade. Yet if we follow the logic of defending one's property rights, such arguments ring hollow. After all, it might be said that the worker also has a 'property right' over their labour power, that is, their principal means to a livelihood. Indeed the creation of legislation on workers' redundancy rights in many countries emerged on acceptance of the principle that a worker has some modicum of 'ownership' in the job. It is a job or job task that becomes redundant, not principally a person. If we accept that the worker has a property right over their labour power and effort, then to uphold this right one might insist they be free to negotiate the terms on which it is provided. True, it could be countered that upon entering the contract of employment, the employee hands over this labour power to the possession of the employer for a finite period of time, therefore the employee's right to dispose of their property has been traded off for receipt of financial remuneration. This empowers the employer to dispose of such purchased labour capacity in any (legal) way they see fit.

But such argumentation would be unsatisfactory, for if anything the exchange of labour power is more akin to a lease than to full ownership rights: in fact it is more helpful to think about the exchange as similar to a tenancy agreement between a landlord and tenant. The tenant receives the property for their use, but such usage is highly constrained by the landlord's ultimate right to ownership. Should the property be 'misused' in some way, perhaps through unruly student house parties which destroy fixtures and fittings, the landlord will likely reassert their property rights. Similarly, as we have seen, an employee may experience that their labour property, hired out to the employer, can be misused in some way, thereby encouraging a reassertion of their rights and sanction. Of course the landlord of a house, as a static and inanimate object, has the advantage, as any tenancy agreement will demonstrate, of being able to specify rigorously the obligations and responsibilities of how the tenant may use the property. The employee, in contrast, in an open-ended employment relationship, faces a more dynamic and uncertain exchange and can only specify some basic conditions on which the labour is supplied at the outset, without knowing how it will change at some point in the future. This of course means that it is all the more possible that disputes will arise. Both worker and employer can then theoretically argue about a form of property interference and it seems unreasonable to give primacy to employer rights over others in this case, at least in any way that encroaches on the employee's ability to uphold the terms of the deal. Admittedly, the employer has the force of law behind them, but in terms of logic there is simply no reasonable defence of an employer's property rights as a valid countenance to strike action.

Another argument for those who would deny the legitimacy of conflict is the disruption that such actions impose upon 'innocent bystanders' or the 'ordinary public'. No doubt when junior doctors strike, Rupert Murdoch's reporters will be on hand to provide plenty of airtime to the sick and needy when operations are cancelled. Such presentations can be powerful in their effect, often portraying those striking as a narrow interest group with a selfish agenda that unfairly disrupts a community by 'holding management (or the public) to ransom'. It may often be accompanied by claims that the strike is a product of an unrepresentative minority, thereby raising the question about undemocratic power. But these do not enlighten an analysis or further an understanding of the striking behaviour in the first place. Let us recall the chapter's opening with our fictional, but plausible, account of a company in crisis. Shareholders are upset and their agents, the management, must see to it that the returns on investment improve. Having identified the shareholders' grievance (falling profits), the managers take it upon themselves to identify and attribute the source of the problem on labour costs. Given that managers are employed to look after money, not individual workers, they mobilise what might be called an 'investment' or 'capital strike'. The message in this case is clear: workers either offer concessions or suffer job loss and the denial of their livelihood. How different is this behaviour to the definition of a strike earlier? That is a withdrawal, or threat thereof, of investment by employers in response to their grievance (an unsatisfactory rate of profit) or to enforce a particular demand (like a concession on wages and greater flexibility). Yet whereas the striking worker receives no income or social insurance, striking capital can at least earn interest in a bank account or reinvest elsewhere. Further, unlike the temporary nature of a worker strike, an employer investment strike may become a permanent affair through sackings, layoffs or plant and job relocations (often with little or minimal notice to those affected).

These 'investment' or 'capital-led' strikes are rarely the subject of outraged editorial commentaries in the *Daily Mail*; Billy Bragg or Ian Prowse do not write starry-eyed songs about them; nor do employment relations textbook chapters on conflict display much interest in such strikes engendered by employers' action. Yet if the employer 'investment strike' is of significant proportions, its effects resonate for months, years, indeed decades following closures, as the Rust Belt of the American Mid-West and the deindustrialisation of the Ruhr testify. The associated number of 'working days lost', a favoured measure of the strike analyst when workers elect to engage in a temporary stoppage, is far more substantive in the case of an employer investment strike than that of a worker-led one. Most worker-led strikes, for all the inconvenience they may cause, are ephemeral affairs, rarely lasting more than one day. Despite the consequences of corporate or investment strikes, it seems less fashionable to lambast narrow interest groups of shareholders for holding workforces, their families and even their communities to 'ransom'. Politicians, far from castigating company directors as 'the enemy within' (as Thatcher did on the National Union of Mineworkers (NUM) in the UK) or 'a peril to national safety' (as did Reagan on the Professional Air Traffic Controllers Organization (PATCO) in the US), will hurry forth with generous tax breaks, grants and subsidies to appease the corporate strikers. Nor is one likely to hear calls for greater legal regulation of the investment strike in defence of the 'national interest', for if governments interfered in the internal affairs of the investment withdrawal, as they do with unionised disputes, cries of state totalitarianism would likely ensue.

▬▬▬ strikes: industrial democracy in action?

Before concluding this short chapter, we might, aside from addressing the jaundiced treatment of industrial action, be somewhat bolder and suggest that worker-led strikes are a fundamental freedom in any democratic society: a human right of organisation and expression. Perhaps a very simple way to think about this is as follows: imagine for a moment that you are marooned on a remote island, with only your humble authors and some coconut trees for company (this may seem unpalatable, but we can be good company). However, the island is not just any island; rather, it appears to have some very unusual properties. As soon as we wash upon the shore, an unseen voice from the sky-blue heavens above us booms:

> Welcome to my island, Coconut Island! Hear ye my commands. Henceforth, I shall, in my infinite wisdom, appoint a leader to rule over you and control the collection and distribution of this island's coconuts. This leader shall not be chosen from amongst you, but shall be imposed by me and shall rule at their discretion until they choose otherwise.

And so it goes. Through a puff of smoke, our first leader, as if by magic, is conjured before our eyes. Before us stands Mother Teresa, that kind old nun who cared for the sick and needy throughout her sainted life. As a result our time on Coconut Island is not so bad; Mother Teresa joins equally in the collection and distribution of coconuts and appears to have an egalitarian style. This harmonious situation passes peacefully for several months until we awake one morning to find Teresa gone, our previous day's store of coconuts unceremoniously cracked open and their shells laid waste. We hear a slurping sound behind a nearby bushel of pinnate leaves, whereupon we investigate to uncover none other than Kim Jong-un, the supreme leader of the Democratic People's Republic of Korea, guzzling the residues of milk from the last remaining coconut. The voice booms through the clouds above us: 'Hear ye, hear ye', it intones, 'I have appointed a new leader to rule amongst you!' Times are tough. Whilst Kim sits back and enjoys the balmy sun, he forces us to collect the daily supply of coconuts, which he then unilaterally distributes, conveniently taking the lion's share for himself. After two years of toil and sweat, we awake one morning to find that Kim too has departed overnight to seek his fortunes elsewhere. As before, the voice booms, a leader is appointed and from behind the covering of some long palm grass, steps Mahatma Gandhi. An upturn in our fortunes, as Mahatma organises coconut production in much the same way as Mother Teresa. But, as before, Gandhi stays a while and then arbitrarily leaves. The cycle, over which we have no control, continues: sometimes we find ourselves in luck (Florence Nightingale), sometimes we get a raw deal (Joseph Goebbels).

Until one day, a bottle washes up on the shore. Curiously there is a message in the bottle, written by someone called Sting, who writes that across the sea lies another island. Sting claims that on this island, the leaders and their preference for coconut collection and distribution are not appointed by some unforeseen random force. Rather, amongst the island's populace, candidates propose themselves as leaders with their own ideas around coconut production and distribution, compete in an election, upon which the winning candidate rules for a period of five years. However, should the leader dissatisfy his or her constituents, the populace may withdraw their support and call a fresh election from which a new leader emerges. As Sting's message concludes with a call to all finders of the bottle to join this coconut paradise, we realise the democratic deficit on Coconut Island is real: our leaders are appointed randomly and whilst occasionally a gem is appointed, the process is so random that we could equally happen upon Idi Amin or Pol Pot. While it holds that on Sting's island we may not be blessed in getting a Nightingale or Gandhi, we would exercise some control over our leader and how they behave by virtue of our voting sanction. We know which island we would rather take our chance on... In the dead of night, as our most recently appointed leader Ken Dodd and his unelected cabinet of Diddymen sleep, we're persuaded to escape and secretly cast off on our coconut-constructed raft with the aim of reaching Sting's island of representative democracy.

Exhibit Box 6.1   Escape from Coconut Island: Ken Dodd outlines his latest strategy to increase coconut productivity.

Credit: Photo by B. Powell/Express/Getty Images

If you think about the workplace, which island is the contemporary employment relationship more like? Apart from a very small and relatively insignificant number of worker cooperatives, most workplaces are in fact more akin to Coconut Island: we have little influence or control over who our bosses are, despite the great significance they hold over our daily working lives and the decisions they make about the production and distribution of wealth. Due to random fortune we can be lucky and get a good manager or we can be unlucky and get an awful leader, someone who may pursue, at will, an investment strike against us at any moment in time and, in the process, potentially leave us on the scrapheap. Given the structure of social relations in our societies, it is highly unlikely you will ever be afforded the opportunity to elect your boss. But it is not inconceivable that the relative randomness and uncertainty over who controls your employment experience can be moderated, not by the luxury of a vote, but by the sanction of labour withdrawal, best exemplified in the use, or threatened use, of the collective workers' strike. Without this capacity to withdraw and regulate labour supply, the employer need not fear sanctions and need not be particularly responsive to people's needs. They may, like a Roman patrician commanding the plebeians, proceed to order the production and distribution in whatever way they seek. The freedom to withdraw, or limit labour, acts in many ways as an employment relations equivalent to the democratic vote in pure political relations. It is a sanction allowing workers to minimise the random and sometimes degrading effects of their employers' management style, ensuring that their voice is less likely to fall on deaf ears.

conclusion

Worker-led strikes are an exemplar of employment relations conflict. Involving mass organisation by individual workers in pursuit of collective demands, they are difficult to organise, costly and often uncertain in outcome. A strike can secure great gains for the workers, but it can also secure great losses. The industrial strike has been in decline, but this has not stemmed the fireworks of controversy over the purpose, function or legitimacy of a strike in modern society. To be sure strikes can be disruptive and damaging on many different levels. The construction of workplaces where employees never felt the need to strike would in all probability be a highly desirable objective. Nonetheless we have attempted to look at some of the arguments invariably raised about the nature and impact of strikes. We have found many of them concerned with undermining the right to strike to be partial and unsatisfactory. Strikes not only reflect the 'structural antagonism' in employment relations, they are also a phenomenon both parties to the relationship engage in. It seems to us that an employer would soon cry foul of any government that prevented their freedom and capacity to withdraw their investment resources as required, challenging such regulation as undemocratic and totalitarian. Likewise, the case for democracy applies to the employee who must surely be entitled to the same rights in withdrawing their labour should they deem it necessary. Employers may charge that such freedom risks the viability of the business as an ongoing concern, placing jobs and future employment at risk. However, given that workers (and their union representatives) can reasonably be assumed to be rational agents, it seems unlikely they would strike if such possibilities were a very real outcome; no worker would put 'their' employment and livelihood at risk. Workers could only strike in such circumstances due to incomplete information and a mistaken judgement of the real standing of the firm. If this was the case, employers could simply rectify such outcomes by – to quote Walter Reuther, a leading American union leader from the mid-20th century – 'opening the books' and allowing workers free and independent access to the information often jealously guarded by management. The often-used claim about the irrationality of worker strikes is no better a justification for some real industrial democracy and participation.

7

Having a Say: Earnings and Working Time

The notion that people should have a say in matters which concern them and affect their work stretches back to biblical times and preoccupied the discussions of Greek philosophers like Aristotle, Plato and others. As in the Monty Python movie *Life of Brian*, philosophers of the biblical era mulled over the meaning of citizenship and democracy – or in the case of Monty Python, how the 'People's Front of Judea' might democratise the Roman Empire. Today, it seems to be common sense that workers should speak up when there are problems which need to be brought to the attention of their employer. As Richard Hyman (2015: 12) has observed: '[It is] impossible to be a free citizen in the public sphere but a slave in the workplace. Democracy [cannot] end outside the factory gates: workers [are] stakeholders in the firm...and must have industrial citizenship rights.' At the same time, the notion and practice of employee voice has proved contentious. As you might now realise from prior chapters, voice is part of an employment relationship that is riddled with antagonism over the distribution of rewards and effort. How this antagonism might be 'worked out' (as John, Paul, George and Ringo put it) is political and often determined by power: in this context, the capacity of one voice to prevail over, or indeed quell, others.

Employee voice is often understood to concern the ways and means through which workers attempt to have a say and influence issues that affect their work (Wilkinson et al., 2014). As we saw in Chapter 2, the balance between 'voice, equality and efficiency' has been presented (by Budd, 2004) as an important way to view employment relations outcomes. Voice channels can involve a variety of mechanisms, some more meaningful or equal than others, and can encompass employee behaviours that contribute to performance and/or challenge management authority. So voice captures both the cooperative and conflictual aspects of employment relations addressed in the previous two chapters. But why is voice so important? For a start, the workplace is where we spend much of our lives doing things under the direction of others. Given this, workers need a voice to express their concerns and creativity, while employers should provide them with the opportunity and the encouragement to do so.

So far so good. But problems arise, as you probably understand by now, because most workplaces can be fraught with tension and most businesses (at least in the private sector) are designed to produce profits and wealth for the firm's owners, not to provide employee voice. This stark reality in turn is often echoed in the sentiments of employers who simply view workers as a disposable means to a profitable end and see worker involvement, participation and voice as irksome or unnecessary. As one manager commented to us during our research on employee involvement and participation, 'Why do I need to think Joe from stores has anything to offer me? If he did, he would not be Joe from stores.' In many ways this is a depressing view of how managers can and do view and treat people. In fact, Henry Ford once complained, 'When I want a pair of hands I get a human being as well.' Other so-called leaders can be equally disparaging of their subordinates, as Herman Wouk reminds us when recounting his personal adventures as a naval steward on a Second World War destroyer in his 1952 novel *The Caine Mutiny* (later, a successful movie). In one part, Wouk reminisces about leadership and the lack of voice, when asking, 'Do we really want organisations designed by geniuses to be run by idiots?' Mind you, that his story ended in a mutiny by the crew suggests that there is a message in there when organisations renege on their commitment to share information with workers. Nevertheless, in many prescriptive management and business texts, the implicit assumptions of Fredrick Taylor still find an echo, fostering assumptions that brain work should be the preserve of managers only, while others, the workers as subordinates, follow orders. Prescriptions of command, control and power prevail in the ethos and structure of many a modern workplace, from the call centres you dread contacting when you have a broadband connectivity issue to the production cycle of that Big Mac or doner kebab you later regret eating on the way home from a nightclub on a Thursday night. In many everyday work environments, workers are instructed with extensive detail outlining minuscule elements of their work task, with little say or opportunity to deviate or offer creative input.

Despite some employers' best efforts to minimise worker input, the reality is that the employment relationship is a two-way thing: employees invariably have their own concerns and will seek to realise them to the best of their ability. As these sometimes complement as well as compete with those of employers, the notion and practice of employee voice is contentious. In this chapter, we will consider these issues further. First, we will begin with an overview of voice and think about the ways and means through which employees attempt to have a say and influence over organisational affairs that affect their work. Of course it is all very well and good to talk about voice in the abstract, so we then move to reflect on whether employees actually do have a voice by reviewing some of the 'big ticket' employment relations 'outcomes' of pay and working time. In the same way it would be difficult to discuss a football match without talking about the final score, it is difficult to talk about voice (or indeed the employment relationship) without addressing pay and hours of work. The pay we receive from our work and the time we spend at it are the basic stuff of the wage–effort bargain. It is important to assess how well workers are able to speak up on such matters.

untangling the notion of voice

Whilst employee voice might be desirable, it is worth pointing out that the way it is understood in employment relations and management studies is far from obvious. Meanings and interpretations change over time and space. For example, during the 1960s and 1970s voice was intimately related to the trend in 'worker participation' as a way to address a perceived problem at the time of employee alienation across industry. But worker participation was interpreted in widely different ways: for some, it was aligned with 'job enrichment' and enhanced worker motivation to enable employers to overcome the anomic tendencies of Fordist production. For others, participation was interpreted as 'industrial democracy', based not on solving problems of alienation but as a source of power sharing between workers, often through trade unions, and employers in the making of joint decisions.

The meanings shaping patterns of employee participation are driven in part by a changing social and economic context of the times: increasing worker militancy, industrial conflict and 'profit squeeze' led many to look for alternatives to the slowdown in economic growth of the 1970s. By the 1980s, 1990s and 2000s, however, as the context became characterised by declining union influence and resurgent employer power, the tone of debate shifted to considerations of 'employee involvement' as a way to improve productivity within increasingly competitive markets. Against a background of diminishing labour power and collective mobilisation, definitions of employee voice became colonised by a new managerial lexicon in which voice needed to demonstrate value, market performance and commercial worth (Barry and Wilkinson 2016). A further twist can be witnessed in the proposal by

British Prime Minister Theresa May for a voice agenda advocating worker directors on company boards.[30] Many ER scholars, quite rightly, would be sceptical of a prime minister's view of worker directors on company boards, if only because the evidence and history of Conservative Party ideology closely aligns with a unitarist, free-market, neo-liberal view of ER, which has consistently favoured the employer's profit objective over any goals for enhanced labour democracy.

Academic analysis reflects the changing meanings and forms of managerial thinking about employee voice, encapsulated in the fashionable managerial models of 'best-practice HRM' and 'employee engagement' (Dundon and Wilkinson, 2017). These ideas emphasise voice as something that can improve the profitability of the firm through tapping into workers' knowledge. A key enabler of engagement is said to be voice; that is, where employee views are actively encouraged, sought out, listened to, this can make a difference to both worker wellbeing and organisational effectiveness. Yet reflecting the shifting emphasis from participation to involvement, John Purcell (2014) observed that little attention is given to collective institutions of voice, such as trade unions, as an effective conduit for employee contributions. From reading Chapter 4 about actors and Chapter 5 on cooperation, you should probably be able to guess why that is. It is tempting to be dismissive of engagement as just the latest fad in a long line of manipulative management techniques. But engagement and voice identify the importance of workers' ideas and knowledge as a source of value extraction for employers. Many workers in their jobs are enthusiastic, energetic and creative, but for all the bluster about engagement, many managers choose to ignore them. Rather, they opt to hold on to the remaining residue of what French and Raven (1959) described as 'authority power', exercised through hierarchical command rather than 'personal efficacy' through respect, knowledge or expert judgement. The expansion of employee engagement practices does not necessarily equate with more voice. Team working, for example, may well be seen as offering workers a degree of autonomy about certain things they might previously have been denied, yet that does not eliminate tensions, antagonism or conflict within the employment relationship. In fact it has been remarked that as management search for new ways to control employee effort, the result has been employees becoming more and more silent (Donaghey et al., 2011). First, managers can control and shape the agenda, which effectively manages employees out of the voice channel. Or second, employees become silent in protest against the encroachment of managerial control over more and more aspects of their working lives. In this way voice becomes like spitting in the wind, or what Wilkinson (2015) terms 'trickle-up voice', which can lead to workers becoming demoralised as management pays scant attention to resolving issues, as illustrated in Table 7.1 below, on 12 ways to stifle employees' voice (adapted from Wilkinson, 2016):

Table 7.1   12 ways to stifle the employees' voice

Deaf ear syndrome.
Kicking into the long grass.
I know best/ I can't change….
Bring me solutions not problems.
Only tell me good news.
Tell someone who cares.
Trickle up voice.
Let me get back to you on that
SEP (Someone else's problem).
Please do not reply.
Issues left in procedure and never answered
Reprisals: kill the messenger

Source: adapted from Wilkinson 2016

Indeed, many managers themselves can feel threatened by the thought of empowering workers because it risks removal of their power and status. As one supervisor reported to us in a fieldwork study about worker voice, 'Bosses are bosses and kick ass; workers should be there to take orders.'

Given the variability in interpretations of voice, a useful way to evaluate different guises of involvement and participation is to think in terms of the depth, scope, level and forms of voice (drawing from work with Marchington et al., 1992). By *depth*, one should consider the extent to which workers (or their representatives) share influence with management in decision making. If workers have little or no say over managerial actions then their voice is pretty 'shallow', whereas in contrast, 'deep' voice enables workers to meaningfully contribute to the final decision-making outcome in some way. *Scope* expresses the range of issues addressed within a particular voice arrangement, and a process which is narrow on this dimension allows management to define certain matters as reserved for their prerogative, ensuring that only minor matters, sometimes disparagingly termed 'tea and toilet roll' issues, are available for employee influence. In contrast, voice with a wide scope would allow worker contributions to extend to input on more strategic matters, like how to use new technologies, negotiate pay or jointly decide on hours of work. In the Brazilian-based company Semco, for instance, its chief executive Ricardo Semler talks of a new wave of voice: moving from telling people what to do, to empowering them to understand how and why they need to start making their own decisions, including decisions on what to pay themselves and when to take their holidays. Staff know they can go home when they feel like, or work from home instead of in the office. Employees don't have a specific work station and 'hot desk', which is thought to support inclusion and engagement across teams and groups. Of course, being told to work at home or informed that you are now empowered or engaged may be somewhat ironic, so more critical reflection later, but the example illustrates that there are interesting and novel ideas about the depth and scope of employee participation. The *level* of employee voice concerns the hierarchical position within the firm at which voice is articulated: ranging from high (such as the company board room) to low (such as team or individual task level on the production floor). Finally, *form* refers to the actual methods used to enable voice and is typically thought of as being either direct or indirect. The former refers to instances where the contact is between individuals or small groups of employees and their immediate manager, whereas in the latter instance, that exchange is mediated through an employee representative such as a shop steward who acts as an agent for a larger group of workers.

However, there are many situations where management supports for employees to express their voice are absent and interaction with workers is lacking. In such situations employees may have to search for ways to articulate their voice that are more akin to protest, operating outside employer provisions for voice. For example, when we studied a company called 'Mini Steel', workers articulated their voice over workplace grievances through a rogue employee known as the 'Scarlet Pimpernel' who engaged in guerrilla-style graffiti around the plant. The workers also used public campaigns targeting the company's personnel director, who refused to recognise their trade union, portraying him on 15-foot billboard posters in a macho style as Arnold Schwarzenegger's uncompromising *Terminator*, and on other posters as an owner lacking empathy and compassion, with his face superimposed on the Tin Man from *The Wizard of Oz* (having no heart). Other interesting consequences of workforce reactions to a perceived lack of voice include the 'frying burger game'. Royle (2000) reports incidents from a McDonald's outlet where workers would engage in their own form of 'sabotage' or 'protest', in part because management would use the franchise status of the restaurant to bypass European work-council arrangements. The employees, who were slightly out of sight of customers and supervisors, typical in a very busy restaurant, would play a game that involved see-ing who could dispense, by working the hardest in hot kitchen condi-tions, drips of bodily sweat from their foreheads or arms while frying the burger patty. The aforementioned burger would be processed with scientific management efficiency, including lettuce, cheese and the annoying pickled gherkin all placed in its bread bun and duly wrapped, dropped by the employee into the heated shoot for the next customer in the queue. The winner of the game was the one who could complete as many 'sweaty hamburgers' in a set timeframe. The object of such a game is not to harm the customer *per se*. It may not even be to resist management. It may, however, be a way for employees to ameliorate degrading working conditions and a coping mechanism for workers to pass the time in a less-than-pleasant employment relationship, or a work regime with a lack of employee involvement and participation in management decisions.

What one can take from this medley of 'depth, scope, level and form' is that whilst employees can have a voice of different sorts and types, a crucial issue is whether that voice matters or if it falls on management's deaf ears? If worker influence over the outcomes of the employment relationship is marginal or non-existent, then the extent to which employees have a voice that actually matters is questionable and kick-back, protest or sabotage may be a rational and logical consequence of a specific employment relationship. It is not just about the taking part, having some 'winning' outcomes matters too. So let us examine this further about voice over pay and hours of work.

voice and pay

You will probably agree that there are likely to be few workers who would not want a voice over their pay. What you earn from your employment relationship is clearly one of the more important aspects of the exchange, and former US President Barack Obama thinks so too. A White House summit on the 'future of worker voice' brought together employees, union and community leaders, business executives, policy advocates and government officials. At the summit Obama remarked, 'Wages need to rise more quickly. We need jobs to offer the kind of pay and benefits that let people raise a family. And in order to do that, workers need a voice."[31]

Of interest, at the opening of the White House Summit, Obama is introduced in a passionate and warm address by union activist Terrance Wise, a second generation fast food worker. At the summit Terrance meets his mother, Joann, a first generation fast food worker, for the first time in ten years. When Obama takes the microphone, he explains why they haven't met in ten years: 'Neither of them make enough money to be able to afford to travel much, so this is the first time Terrence and Joann have seen each other in 10 years...because they don't earn enough to be able to just hop on a plane and visit each other...Their story describes why workers need a voice.'[32] Of course it may be that such an event is more spin than real; after all, in reality, presidents and prime ministers can more easily pass laws to mandate employee voice or ensure worker directors have access to the same information and participation as other corporate directors. Indeed, many employees lack a direct voice in determining their wages and salaries as most are subject to the arbitrary whims of market and employer authority, becoming essentially price-takers rather than price-makers. In times when the labour market is buoyant and employers compete with each other for labour, this may not seem so bad and indeed go unnoticed. Where competition among managers for labour is so strong that they have no alternative but to offer more money, an individual may come to directly negotiate terms and conditions of their hire. Those fortunate individuals with in-demand skills can usually play the market and ensure their pay demands are met. The rest of us, the vast majority, have to make do with what we get, perhaps hoping that a rising tide of full employment will lift all boats.

Yet there is a recognition that the relationship between high levels of employment and wage pressures has changed in recent years – due to changes in the functioning of labour markets and the rise in non-standard employment discussed below – that a huge drop in unemployment is needed to provide upward pressure on earnings (Haldane, 2015). If you consider the recovery in employment levels from the Great Recession, workers' wages have, in the main, remained pretty stagnant in countries likes the US, UK and other developed economies. The economist Alan Manning (2015) has observed that not too long ago a recovering labour market in Britain would have led trade unions to voice demands for higher wages and threaten strikes if their voice fell on deaf ears. Union officials, in discussion with workplace representatives and the wider membership, would formulate a pay claim, put it to management and negotiate a deal which would often have industry-wide significance. In such situations union bargaining may even raise the pay of non-union members as other forms and sectors follow industry pay-setting norms. With the weakening of workers' power as a countervailing voice and the erosion of collective bargaining as a pay-setting mechanism, however, it is now the employers' voice that frequently calls the shots on pay. This trend is evident when we examine wage patterns in countries like the United States, Japan and Germany.

In these cases, we have actually seen a 'decoupling' of pay from productivity in recent decades; that is, American, Japanese and German workers are producing more stuff over time, but their pay is not necessarily keeping pace with their increased output. For various institutional reasons, workers in these companies lack the necessary muscle to make a claim on the fruits of their labour. Employers are just too powerful. Indeed the diminution of collective worker voice, exemplified by the weakening of joint pay setting in many countries, is now well accepted in many quarters as an important driver of rising income inequality. As workers lose the capacity to negotiate pay or enforce their pay demands, their employers simply transfer the firm's income into the pockets of higher executive pay and shareholder returns (Western and Rosenfeld, 2011).

Structural change in the contemporary labour market also has implications for worker voice over pay. Labour markets across a number of developed economies are said to increasingly exhibit an 'hourglass figure', that is, an occupational structure polarised between expanding ranks of high-skilled jobs at the top end of the hierarchy and low-skilled jobs at the bottom (Sissons, 2011). The number of jobs requiring mid-skilled workers, like tradespeople and machine operatives, is shrinking. For the latter, the growth of technology and automation in the workplace means many of those types of jobs that were prominent 30 years ago are no longer required or have been 'off-shored'. The London School of Economics anthologist David Graeber (2013) posits that the growth in higher-status jobs, the 'new professions' of expanding 'white-collar' and managerial CEO jobs, merely represents an increase in 'bullshit jobs': their only social function, he claims, is to create positions designed to make these workers identify with the perspectives and sensibilities of the ruling class, and in so doing devalue the efforts of real, productive workers like bin collectors, nurses or tube drivers. Whatever the (dubious) social value of marketing strategists, CEOs, KPMG partners or business school professors, one of the more interesting developments in recent years is the use of variable or performance-related pay ratings and systems. For some workers such schemes are welcome and offer some input over pay. Where workers have had a genuine say about agreeing their targets and subsequent assessment, such schemes can offer a degree of control over earnings insofar as superior performance is recognised and rewarded. Yet variable pay systems are often Kafkaesque in their application; that is, they are purposely complex with employee input into the process limited or non-existent, and the assessment over rating and reward opaque. In these cases employees are subjected to the whims of their supervisors' proficiency in grading performance. In Yahoo, for example, it has been alleged that the supervisors who make the evaluations are forced to adhere to a 'rank and yank' system:[33] that is, higher-rated employee rewards must be offset by reducing staff to balance costs. When employees do come to understand how such systems work, they can be quite creative in finding ways to game the system (e.g. conspiring to inflate results to secure a bonus or escape the axe). Mars' (1982) classic sociological study of workplace cheating, for example, recounts how Blackpool tram drivers would go to all sorts of extremes to meet targets on travel times, which often involved speeding up to get to destinations earlier, to then secure unscheduled breaks. However, for most workers, gaming a system is less an exercise in employee voice and more a response to unequal rules that can affect their pay and earnings. When viewed in this context, game playing is logical and highly rationale when employees have their voice constrained or denied.

Voice over pay can be completely absent for the many working in relatively low-paid and insecure jobs, typically with no union representation. Whereas an expansion in demand for high-skilled jobs tended to pull up real wages in recent decades, a rise in the demand for low-skilled workers has been coupled with real-wage stagnation, because there have simply been more people queuing up for the low-skilled jobs on offer. With a willing pool of applicants for every low-skilled opening, employers are not incentivised to raise wages. One worrying development associated with low pay employment relationships is the rise of in-work poverty. Even in Germany, known for its low unemployment and successful export model, in-work poverty has become especially visible, where the effect of jobs moving to Eastern Europe, and workers arriving from new member states has put wages under pressure in transport, hotel and cleaning industries. In Britain, it used to be that worklessness was the prime determinant of poverty but now it is more likely to be low-waged work (MacInnes et al., 2015). Unless these workers find some way to have employers listen to their voice, either through organising collectively or legal supports, they are like to remain trapped in low-pay work and many depend on welfare benefits to make ends meet.

In terms of voice a further development here is how the low-paid can use wider, often social-media-based campaigns to exercise voice and secure favourable outcomes. When B&Q attempted in 2016 to compensate for the rise in the minimum wage by cutting Sunday and over-time premiums, an online campaign by one of its workers led to the company reversing its practice.[34] There is an important point here. Even in market situations of evident employer power and union exclusion (B&Q is a celebrated non-union company), alternative channels, including political processes, to leverage worker voice emerge that promote social fairness. Ultimately, developments of this sort and campaigns for living wages and the like are important, because not only do the low-paid suffer from being caught up in such poorly paid jobs but so too does everyone else in society. Invariably it is citizens who end up subsidising low-wage employers through various forms of in-work benefits and tax reliefs for low-paid workers. In the United States for example, taxpayers contribute approximately $1 billion a year to help pay workers *just* at McDonald's alone, because so many of their employees rely on public assistance programmes like food stamps and medical care supports (Jacobs et al., 2015).

It may be helpful to recall at this point the advice of Adam Smith who wrote that 'where wages are high, we shall always find the workmen more active, diligent, and expeditious than where they are low' (cited in Routh, 1989: 97). Some economists have put forward a hypothesis known as the 'fair wage-effort hypothesis' (Akerlof and Yellen, 1990), which proposes that if the actual wage is lower than the workers' notion of the fair wage, they will withdraw their effort in proportion. Greenberg (1990) found that employee thefts were significantly high in situations where management imposed pay cuts without providing adequate information or showing remorse. With many low-pay workers lacking voice to challenge and contest an objectionable state of affairs they may adjust to inequities through subterranean misbehaviour. Of course, in the low-pay sector, the sticky-fingered checkout operator may simply be a latter day Robin Hood, appropriating unjustly expropriated wealth in the absence of institutional supports for their voice. As noted in Chapter 3, many workers struggle to receive from their employer the wages they have legitimately earned. One study in the US reported the problem of employer 'wage theft' to be 'endemic' (Meixell and Eisenberry, 2014). Each year, the value of wages not paid to employees by corporations amounts to more than twice the money stolen from 'bank, petrol station and convenience store robberies combined': the Economic Policy Institute claim that wage theft has deprived workers of $50 billion a year. Low trust begets low trust and the silencing of employees' voice in the low-paid sector simply fosters dysfunctional and socially unjust outcomes.

Society is recognising that the low paid lack a real voice in these matters and thus has sponsored policy interventions around 'minimum wage' laws and 'living wages' to close the gap. The impact of such measures is often controversial, not least for reasons of business affordability, consumers' costs and employment, but even in terms of the occasional public relations disasters that undermine employers' image: like the Church of England who, despite their proclamations of support for a 'living wage', were found, rather ungodly, not to be paying it themselves.[35] Of course, whether such measures protect those at the vulnerable end of the labour market is questionable. One recent report by the UK government's Migration Advisory Committee (2014) found employment rules like minimum wage laws were either not being properly enforced or were flouted by employers, and this was particularly likely in the informal sector where migrant labour is common. Statistically, employers could expect a minimum wage compliance visit from statutory inspectors just once in 250 years, the report found, which means that at current rates they would face prosecution for breaching labour laws only every million years. Now the minimum wage does appear to be observed by many employers, but the problem for voice is still significant. One can reasonably doubt whether the law in itself will provide the low-paid with the voice they need on pay. The crucial thing about the law is that it has to be accessed and enforced and this can be problematic for several reasons. First, where enforcement from the state is partial and under resourced, as is frequently the case in these times of austerity, avoidance of the law by unscrupulous employers can (and does) occur. Second, the very workers most reliant on the law to ensure minimum wage entitlements are often the very workers who lack the knowledge, time and financial resources to access those same statutory supports. A poverty of voice may well reproduce poverty in pay.

voice and working time

For the majority of us, how long we'll be expected to work along with when we get our holiday entitlements are among the most pertinent elements of the employment contract. If you recall the problem of 'indeterminacy' in Chapter 4 – that is, the difficulty in specifying exactly how much effort our contract expects us to perform – the length of time we are expected to be at work is a prominent surrogate used by employers to define expectations of performance to be provided. So many workers sell their time to an employer as much as they sell their potential to work. From the perspective of the worker, having some voice over the timing, tempo and duration of their labour would seem desirable. This is particularly so if we accept the idea, common to economists, that work is something of a necessary evil or 'disutility'. Work is a 'disutility' for to labour is to make a sacrifice of one's leisure and comfort, and wages are a kind of compensation for such sacrifices.

However, to while away one's hours in labour may not be innately repellent in itself. Bricklayers, artists, coffee baristas and school teachers feel immensely proud of their work achievements, as do others across a very diverse range of jobs. Indeed, many 19th century philosophers – including Karl Marx and William Morris – questioned whether to toil away the hours was inherently disagreeable or whether much depended on the social relations under which our work effort is performed (Spencer, 2009). This is plausible. When one works with autonomy, at a time and speed of one's choosing to erect, say, a garden shed or a child's tree house, the elbow grease involved can be fulfilling and rewarding. Yet to give up one's hours at the discretion of another, for a purpose over which one has no control, to create a product or service which lacks intrinsic meaning or is for the wealth of others, is likely to stir feelings of dissatisfaction and resentment. In the contemporary employment relationships that most labour under, the latter outcome is probably more common. This suggests then that under circumstances where work is an unavoidable disutility, or at least as one among a number of life's competing priorities, enabling employees to have a voice over their hours of labour is important. This is even recognised in the 'work–life balance' literature and espoused as best practice. Perhaps the work–life balance term is unfortunate, however, insofar as it implicitly elides the fact that work is a major part of our life and not something separate. One can be tempted to infer an underlying political assumption at work here: 'life' is treated as something belonging to the employee, while the 'work' side is a separate sphere over which we should have no intrinsic interest as it is assumed to be owned by the employer. Invariably, too, the focus of such debate is often on the culture of long hours and very little consideration given to work–life *im*balance driven by underemployment – stemming from too few hours or zero hours work arrangements – which can restrain one's ability to enjoy life's activities. To talk about underemployment, however, as a source of work–life imbalance raises political implications about how contemporary labour markets are organised and whose present structure often suits the powerful. Work–life balance to address long hours can more easily be resolved through marginal tinkering at the edges of employment practice and then presented as the cutting edge of sophisticated HRM.

Whatever the underlying focus of fashionable discourse, it is reasonable that workers in selling their labour should have the freedom to pursue work and non-work lives successfully, without pressures from one undermining the satisfactory experience of the other. Recent decades have seen workers exercising voice on these matters, using formal legislative support to secure flexitime and leave entitlements. Of course we are talking here about an employment relationship: employers similarly have expectations and requirements over when they need to schedule labour. Employers are keenly interested in time, particularly as it relates to patterns of 'labour flexibility' and relative costs of different working patterns. From the outset, employers have a great deal of influence over working hours by specifying hours associated with job vacancies, shift patterns and demands for overtime. Yet employers do not have it all their own way. In countries like Germany, France and Britain, working time is often a prominent feature of industry and workplace negotiations between employers and unions. How such competing voices over the hours of employment are reconciled, whether one party's voice will prevail over others or whether compromise is struck, will of course hinge on the balance of power between the employer and employee as well as accepted norms of fairness and legitimacy previously mentioned. Even though hours of work have tended to drop throughout the 20th century, as technological change, rising productivity, union power and legislative reform have taken hold, the accommodation of employers' and employees' voices over the contours of the working day remains contested.

What is perhaps the most striking feature of working time in contemporary employment relationships, already alluded to, is the curious spectacle of the 'overworked' and the 'underworked': some people who feel they are working too many hours over and above what they would like, and others who feel they would like to work longer hours but whose job fails to offer those kind of opportunities or indeed because they may have no job at all. Both sets of individuals are essentially victims of a complex and multifaceted set of developments with minimal voice opportunities: changing sectoral dynamics, increased business competition, new technology and the reassertion of employer power over the definition of the working day captured in the euphemism of 'flexibility' which, in practice, often means insecure, irregular or precarious work. The 'long hours culture' features right across occupations, dominating the working time of IT managers, bar staff and those simply cobbling together weekly schedules with multiple part-time and temporary jobs. For some, long hours is presented as a free choice: Goldman Sachs interns working long hours to impress superiors need to be reminded to go home before midnight and not to return before 7am. One cannot help suspect that even for high earning finance brokers the idea of free choice is somehow coerced by peer pressure and cultural expectations. For many, one suspects, long hours are less a choice than a financial necessity, born of the pressures of household debt and simply the need to get by in life. Paid overtime in such circumstances becomes a vital means to supplement low basic rates of pay. For others, long hours can simply be a product of employer power. Through the prevalence of smartphones and email, the demands of work have seeped into non-work time, expanding the supply of unpaid labour. A Trade Union Congress (TUC) analysis claimed that UK workers gave their employers approximately £32 billion of unpaid overtime in 2014, with more than five million workers putting in an average of around eight hours extra of uncompensated work a week.[36] Such unpaid labour can be drawn from any number of sources like mandatory meetings outside of work hours, eating lunch at the desk to complete work, or simply staying an hour or two late to meet deadlines or wrap up tasks. Challenges to employer encroachment on non-work time are relatively muted. If one considers the attention received by alleged 'benefit scroungers' skiving off the back of taxpayers then the relative acquiescence reigning over employers 'sponging off' the free labour of their workforce is striking. There may well be potent sociological forces at play here which enable the relatively powerful in our society to escape attention for such transgressions for reasons of fatalism, ignorance or a capacity to shape dominant social discourse. There also appear to be prevailing social norms around putting in the hours, even if unpaid, because of the cultural approbation of 'working hard'. The concept of 'presenteeism' seems to capture some of this sentiment of workers who are willing to accept long hours because of a desire to demonstrate commitment to superiors. Of course one can paint too benign a portrait: presenteeism also encompasses those workers who feel pressured to put in long hours, even when ill, out of fear of the consequences of not being perceived as a 'willing team player'. Even in these circumstances where workers lack a voice over their working time, they may still assert some control: occasional absenteeism can be used by employees to manage the pressures of work. Within the confines of the working day, employees create spaces for themselves to adapt to the strain of long hours or intensified work by taking their own unauthorised breaks.

If some struggle with long hours, others struggle with the prospect of too few. Such trends are part of wider strata of temporary, part-time and sometimes bogus 'self-employment' brought about by structural change in the labour market. Employers are expanding operating times in manufacturing or extending opening hours into evenings and weekends in the services sector. Such strategies have stimulated greater diversity and fragmentation in the way many of us work because employers mix and match shorter sets of individual work hours within these expanded operating times. This is often cost effective for employers and also lessens their commitment to maintaining a full-time workforce. Interestingly, where hours once worked outside 'standard hours' (like evenings, nights and weekends) were paid at a premium rate in acknowledgement of their greater impact on social or family non-work domains, employers have steadily redefined the working day and are now more likely to pay non-standard hours at non-premium rates. This is perhaps symptomatic of the weakening of workers' collective voice and unions as a counter-vailing power. What we are now seeing in working time is a world that Dolly Parton would struggle to recognise: working nine to five is not the way we make our living. Indeed, in the UK, only a minority now work what was formerly considered a standard workday (full time, Monday to Friday, with no evening or weekend work).

The redefinition of the working day is not straightforward (O'Sullivan et al., 2015). Take, for example, the controversial area of 'zero hour contracts' in the UK or the use of 'on-demand labour' through crowd-sourcing and other digital work task platforms across the globe. While such arrangements may suit the lifestyles and choices of some individuals, they can be emblematic of the disenfranchised worker, a stratum of the workforce utterly exposed to the whims and fancies of their master's voice. This is evidenced in unpredictable working hours, unstable income, lack of say over the scheduling of work hours, insufficient notice when called to work, being sent home during a shift; fear of being penalised by employers for not accepting work, wider life implications like difficulties in accessing credit and social welfare support, as well as reliance on increasingly prominent food banks. Beyond zero hour working, however, is a general growth in non-standard working which has become particularly pronounced in the years since 2008 and the effects of the global recession (O'Sullivan et al., 2015). OECD (2015) evidence demonstrates that atypical jobs have come at the expense of 'standard' permanent employment. The existence of the self-employed and independent contractors, standard-bearers of the new digital work platforms in the 'gig economy' is prominent here. One might be wary of the rhetoric that uncritically treats such trends as 'empowering'. When Uber's CEO claims that the self-employed drivers 'value their independence, the freedom to push a button rather than punch a clock, to drive most of the week or for just few hours', be mindful that Uber management monitor their approval ratings by customers, deactivate their accounts if inactive for 180 days or if approval ratings fall below 4.6 stars. This leads many to suspect that company preference for contractor rather than employee status is simply to avoid wage and hour laws, including the right to the minimum wage and reimbursement of business expenses. In terms of voice, the non-standard worker is likely to be muted by the uncertain, short-term nature of their employment relationships and their lack of bargaining power, whilst for those bogusly categorised as self-employed, they have no voice at all because they are not formally in an employment relationship even where, for all intents and purposes, they are treated as employees.

▰▰▰▰▰ conclusion

Having a voice matters for employees as a means of self-determination (Budd 2004), but whether their contemporary voice is being heard on key elements of the employment relationship, like pay and working time, is debatable with wide variation across the labour market. There are many reasons to be concerned about the existence of a disenfranchised lowly paid precariat and a relatively unchecked increase in employers' labour market power, which for some occupational segments leads to a long-hours culture of unpaid work, and for others not enough hours to make ends meet. It is interesting that our generally discursive overview of voice in these areas is reflected in broader surveys of workers' experiences. In Britain, for example, the Skills and Employment Survey, from the Economic and Social Research Council and the UK Commission for Employment and Skills, reported that workers are feeling less secure and more pressured at work than at any time in the past 20 years (Felstead et al., 2014). Work intensification, meaning the speed of work and pressures of working to tight deadlines, was reported to have also increased since the mid-2000s. Just over half of workers surveyed reported concerns about pay reductions and a loss of say over how their job was done. Almost a third of staff reported anxiety about unfair treatment at work, including being dismissed without good reason and being victimised by management. Interestingly, from the perspective of employee voice, workers were more content and less anxious about job or status loss where employers adopted policies that gave a degree of involvement and decision making at work. Giving workers a voice over the terms and conditions of their employment is therefore valuable from the point of view of how employees experience work. Empowering employees with a voice might also help counter some of the more malign trends we have discussed above, whether that is through enhancing their bargaining rights or ensuring supportive laws are upheld and enforced, and excessive employer power is checked in the workplace. Or, in the words of the Monty Python movie *Life of Brian*, perhaps we should 'always look on the bright side of life (and whistle)', as lest we experience what some South Korean HR managers are keen to encourage their employees to do with their latest staff engagement technique:

> In a large room in a nondescript modern office block in Seoul, staff from a recruitment company are staging their own funerals. Dressed in white robes, they sit at desks and write final letters to their loved ones. Tearful sniffling becomes open weeping, barely stifled by the copious use of tissues. And then, the climax: they

rise and stand over the wooden coffins laid out beside them. They pause, get in and lie down. They each hug a picture of themselves, draped in black ribbon. As they look up, the boxes are banged shut by a man dressed in black with a tall hat. He represents the Angel of Death. Enclosed in darkness, the employees reflect on the meaning of life. The macabre ritual is a bonding exercise designed to teach them to value life…The participants at this session were sent by their employer, human resources firm Staffs. 'Our company has always encouraged employees to change their old ways of thinking, but it was hard to bring about any real difference,' says its president, Park Chun-woong. 'I thought going inside a coffin would be such a shocking experience it would completely reset their minds for a completely fresh start in their attitudes.'[37]

You might wonder whether this is the best strategy for a 'reset' of employee attitudes. Arguably this thinking is not only self-serving and degrading of basic human dignity, it is flawed and contradictory. It is precisely because our lives are so short that we should not be spending them working for organisations that treat people as a means to an end, as expendable pawns with no voice, or those who adopt bizarre strategies that attempt to 'reset' people's thoughts and values as some sort of game of the employer's choosing.

8

Some Concluding Thoughts: ER Education, Immiseration and Automation

introduction

In this the concluding chapter we want to round off our conversation with you about studying ER. We mentioned in the opening chapter we were inspired by Chris Grey's first book in this *Very Short, Fairly Interesting and Reasonably Cheap* series and honoured to extend the spirit of the series by writing about the ER field. You may have noticed that up to this point we have made some critical references to the way you may study the subject, especially if you are enrolled on a business or management type degree at a university business school. In this chapter we wish to add to the observations that Chris Grey made in both his first (2005) and second (2009) editions about studying the subject in the context of a university business school. As part of this reflection we consider some of the dominant approaches to understanding work and employment that frequently populate a business school student's first interaction with the subject areas: organisational behaviour, human resource management and (neo-classical) economics. In particular, we raise some concerns about how these related approaches treat employment, characterising it as either amenable to managerial tinkering or that it can be unproblematically perpetuated without the intrusion of wider societal regulation. The silence around, or avoidance of, social regulation in these perspectives, we propose, reflects a pro-market ideology whose free rein in our society has in part contributed to an unsettling malaise of growing inequality, economic impoverishment and societal discord. Such is the prominence of inequality in our concerns that it also feeds into our final topic for consideration: the important and very contemporary issue of digital technology and automation in the workplace.

▒▒▒▒▒ educating in the business school

Periodically we have reflected on the nature of business school education and its impact on understanding ER. The reason this matters is because it is usually in a business school where work, employment and its management are predominately taught (although university sociology departments continue to make honourable contributions). Over the years our experience of teaching ER within the business school environment has revealed to us tendencies that often pull in different directions. From teaching undergraduate and postgraduate cohorts, we have found how many students view a business school education as simply a means to improve the running of a business or make themselves 'job ready' for a management career. Indeed, many staff in business schools operate from the same prescriptive premise. Under this conceptualisation the study of ER – if it is studied at all – tends to be treated as an instrumental exercise in managing, for example, a disciplinary hearing 'effectively' or knowing the necessary steps to making workers redundant with legal efficacy.

However, there are other pedagogical and philosophical ideas about what a university education should mean, including the learning that takes place within the confines of a business school degree. The antecedents of academic disciplines that occupy business and management schools are often preoccupied with the immediacy of vocational prescription or the practicality of how to run a business or be a better manager. In contrast, many social science scholars within the field of ER reflect an approach very much anchored in the humanities and liberal arts traditions. In this light, ER becomes a field of inquiry in its own right because it contributes to significant areas of economic, political and societal concern. An agenda call for positive change through ER research, teaching and policy involvement has been made by Thomas Kochan, Professor at MIT Sloan. Among other contributions, Kochan (2015) suggests that by engaging in ideas about the future of work relationships we can help develop more informed citizens, improve business practices and shape public policy choices that have many more objectives in addition to market-driven profitability: for example, a public service duty, and charitable and not-for-profit organisational management. And even corporations with a profit motive also have interests related to fairness, equality, justice, and employee and social wellbeing. Thompson and McHugh (2009: 395) further point out that 'Productivity matters to employees as well as managers. It is reasonable to argue that HRM or equal opportunity can be positive for efficiency, as long as this is not the only criterion on which progressive practices are advocated.' The study of ER typically exposes students to challenges not encountered on the more prescriptive managerial or accountancy type modules of a business school degree. Of course, in some quarters, critical social science knowledge may not always be fashionable. One is reminded here of a vice chancellor from a UK university who was reported to have commented that 'society doesn't need a 21-year-old who is a sixth century historian',[38] the implication being that universities should focus on producing functionaries to meet the immediate demands of the market instead of the acquisition and assimilation of knowledge for intellectual pursuit in its own right.

Yet in 1852 Cardinal John Henry Newman, Oxford academic and clergyman, posed the question 'what is a university's purpose?' As you might expect, the answer is not straightforward, although some of the key features about encouraging a probing and questioning style resonate with the spirit of the *Very Short, Fairly Interesting and Reasonably Cheap* series of books. For Newman, a university education ought to advance intellectual pursuits for value in and of themselves. He advanced the idea that a university enables students to think and reason, to compare, to discriminate, to analyse. His template paved the way for many classics faculties and the liberal university approach to education that avoided 'minds born in a narrow specialisation'. The concern has also been a worry to contemporary business school educators. Harvard College Dean Professor Rakesh Khurana has argued that business schools 'face a crisis of irrelevance', suggesting there is a lack of clarity as to 'what an MBA consists of anymore'. Many people spend a fortune purchasing the MBA credential, but in the process they 'don't really learn a lot', he argued. Likewise, the (late) Professor Sumantra Ghoshal of London Business School was more forthright: university business schools have espoused 'bad' theories that have probably contributed to recession and the resulting employment immiseration[39] encountered by many people globally. Indeed, many of the senior executives at the heart of corporate scandals and the global financial crisis were all MBA 'trained' (Dundon, 2014). It remains a wider point of debate that a possible crisis of 'irrelevance' and 'bad theory' has more to do with prescriptive learning outcomes geared to an external purpose that reinforce ideological prejudices around 'the good manager' or fetish 'economic growth' (while, incidentally, saying nothing about the subsequent distribution of the latter's proceeds). This is far removed from the sort of inquisitive open scholarship that Newman sought to inspire, but such trends have impacted directly on the teaching of ER: the long-established Centre for Industrial Relations at Keele University was closed and reconfigured as part of a revamping of the University Business School. As one ER scholar Gregor Gall (2008) observed:

Twenty or more years ago, university departments of industrial relations (and personnel management) began mutating into departments of human resource management and just plain management...Since the Tory onslaught on higher education of the 1980s, universities have been increasingly slanted towards servicing neoliberalism and employers' interests. They've been establishing business and management schools offering degrees in management and human resource management. Any sense in which universities have provided services for the other side of industry – workers and their unions – has all but vanished. [40]

This has created an argument that much of the study about work or management in business schools is frequently entrenched in a one-sided agenda that is orientated around employer objectives. Instead of examining the societal and institutional environment from a multiple stakeholder perspective (a core aspect of the field of ER, as we saw in earlier chapters), the focus of analysis is often directed exclusively towards shareholder value and an ever-increasing profitable return from the way employers can best utilise (exploit) their human resources. Allied to this orientation is an increasing 'psychologisation' of ER (Godard, 2014). Important for how the field is studied has been the contemporary influence of a particular strain of organisational behaviour (OB), that of industrial and organisational (I&O) psychology. As a perspective on employment, I&O psychology, whilst meritorious in its own right, is predominately micro-focused on the individual and largely untouched by any awareness of broader context factors reviewed in Chapter 3: the role of politics, the state, economic ideologies, financialisation or the law, and which we have seen as being so important in understanding the subsequent behaviours of ER actors, processes and outcomes. The psychology approach reduces social relations at work to atomised individuals premised as being engaged in interpersonal exchanges, typically explained through unitarist values assuming that things like engagement or motivation will inevitably be good for all; and any unwillingness for employees to support employer decisions or question managerial authority are seen as inherently problematic. At the level of explanation, this strain of OB remains detached from the wider social structures of society.

Much of the prescriptive psychological reasoning may well suit employer ideology. A psychological perspective chimes with many employers because worker behaviours that conflict with management can be conveniently attributed to individual employee malevolence or workers 'untrained' in the right sort of attitudes. Conflict, in this atomised individual world, can be attributed to varying psychological dispositions amongst the working populace. In such circumstances highly paid executives can legitimise their rewards and status because it is *they* who have been ambitious, motivated and hardworking, unlike their indolent, unenterprising workers whose lower status in the hierarchy reflects a lack of sacrifice and effort. 'Success in life', if measured in wealth at least, becomes less a product of institutional structure or economic positioning than a mere willingness to 'get on one's bike' and graft.

Aside from the ease with which the psychologisation of ER reduces complex class relations to a crass moralism, the approach also sees workplace problems as a failure to identify and apply the 'right technique' in producing 'engaged employees'. This risks consigning, as Mabey and Mayrhofer (2015: 16) recognise, many workplace contradictions to a neutral, apolitical territory, easily malleable by 'best practice' business strategising as a form of social engineering carried out exclusively on the whim of the 'enlightened employer'. In much business schools teaching – management, organisational behaviour or neo-classical economics – there is no mention of an interventionist perspective or shared regulation with a trade union, and so the student is rarely if ever presented with alternative paradigms for critique or other possibilities. It is not just that unilateral employer regulation is taken for granted, however, but that the employer's priorities prevail above all others. Take the issue of employee voice which we addressed in Chapter 7. We saw previously that employee voice in ER is understood as a means by which employees' independent, and often collective, concerns are articulated at work.

Managerialist perspectives, in contrast, including OB, treat voice as an expression of the desire of individuals to communicate information with the primary and often only goal being for the benefit of the organisation (Barry and Wilkinson, 2016). Such perspectives, including HRM and OB, are partial because in treating voice as benefiting the organisation they leave no room for considering voice as a means of challenging management, or as a vehicle for employee self-determination. Employee behaviour is viewed from the unitarist lens we discussed in Chapter 2, where 'what is good for the firm must be good for the worker'. This neglects insight about structural antagonisms, and therefore does not properly consider how employment relations mediate diverse interests between workers and management, giving the former cause to have a voice on their own terms, and in another way creates a power imbalance that limits the capacity of workers to engage in voice. In the ER conceptualisation, adequate voice avenues require active policy intervention through the creation of laws and regulations to sponsor employee voice. In contrast, an OB approach would leave the student to perceive voice with a proviso that its articulation must meet certain prerequisites that 'must' benefit management. Workers do, however, have a legitimate interest in effective voice irrespective of the commercial or business gain. This is a key insight ER brings to the table. It views the employment relationship as one involving multiple stakeholders with contrasting and at times conflicting priorities and interests: defined as we saw by Budd in Chapter 2 as searching for a balance between efficiency, equity and voice. Given the multiplicity of goals, interests and actors, there is no necessary privileging of one group over others. Indeed, if one group is favoured at all, it is the weaker and disadvantaged so as to ensure more socially just outcomes. This is a key advantage of the ER field.

The implications of the ER analysis are often uncomfortable for those in power and call into question their authority and right to manage. There is an interesting parallel here with the wider dominance of a free-market approach amongst many sections of the economics profession. Economics, like psychology or law, is a respected discipline in the ER field and many influential texts are published by leading labour economists. Much of this ER research tends to be developed from the perspective of new institutional or heterodox economics (Marsden, 1999; Grimshaw and Rubery, 2008; Kaufman, 2007; Willman, 2017). Economics is typically the other field in a business school where issues of employment and work are commonly addressed and most students will at some point encounter some variant of Microeconomics 101, with its supply and demand equilibrium and the theory of the firm. However, the dominant orthodoxy within economics as a whole is not heterodox or institutional approaches with an awareness of history, evolution and non-market structures, but is neo-classical economics, with its emphasis on market rationalism, equilibrium-seeking outcomes and measures to predict market efficiency. Like the psychologisation of employment, neo-classical economics provides an ideological justification for minimising social interventions which might otherwise affect an employer's private business activity. Thus when introductory economic textbooks use the model of competitive markets as their standard lens of analysis, they are implying that competitive markets broadly approximate to real-world conditions and produce naturally efficient outcomes.

Students of such approaches are therefore invited to adopt a normative view of the world that assumes there should be a free market, with minimum outside interference, and that this is somehow unquestionably good and the starting point of any analysis. This bias works in other ways too. In its pure form, neo-classical theory assumes that capital and labour earn an amount equal to the value of what they each contribute to the output. Yet such views are silent about how the ownership of different factors of capital are distributed unequally amongst the wider populace. Indeed, equity, in this neo-classical worldview, is always sub-servient to efficiency and 'Pareto optimality': the idea that it is impossi-ble to make any one individual better off without making at least one individual worse off. Minimum wage laws and trade union collective bargaining, the neo-classical economist would argue, create supply-side distortions to the 'free' operation of a market resulting in unemployment by raising the wages of union employees above the free-market equilib-rium rate. This, the neo-classical economists suggest, privileges insiders (union members) at the expense of the unfortunate outsiders (non-union employees), pricing them out of the market.

This argument elevates the idea of 'perfectly competitive' markets as *the* ontological model to understand economic behaviour. In the spirit of education and learning, perhaps you might, if you have the opportu-nity, ask your economics lecturer why the microeconomic course text-book prioritises a model of 'perfect competition', with assumptions of costless information, other factors remaining static or constant, rather than say that of monopsony (where one buyer confronts many sellers) when presenting a treatment of markets? And how willing is that same lecturer to engage in an analysis of the realism of perfectly competitive markets? For example, in a perfectly competitive labour market, if a firm reduces its wages below the equilibrium, its entire workforce should quit because, the model assumes, they can opt to sell their labour at another firm paying the higher market equilibrium rate; that is, 'other things being equal'. Even if the firm's workforce did scarper, this would not concern the employer for they could find replacements by once again offering the market (equilibrium) wage rate. In this model, the relationship between employer and worker is symmetric, there are no concentrations of market power and neither party is more powerful than the other. Each has the equivalent ability to terminate the employment relationship and find another job or another worker (Hill and Myatt, 2010).

However, as we know from Chapter 4, the above depiction is implau-sible in capturing the dynamics of labour market relationships. In real-ity, if a firm reduced its wages just below the equilibrium wage, it would not immediately lose all its workers because of search, information and preference costs. Many workers suffer in a spiral of low wages and precarious work, as finding alternative jobs can be difficult and deter-mined by managers or recruitment agencies, not some invisible free hand guiding between equilibrium-priced jobs. Perhaps one of the most damming indictments of the effects of free market systems is, as we discussed in Chapter 7, the rise of 'in-work poverty' which has now overtaken out-of-work poverty (e.g. McDonald's in the US advising employees how to claim food stamps). The reality is most employers have a high degree of market power over their workforce. As a result, economists like Alan Manning (2005) have argued that a monopsony model of labour markets might not be the rarity that neo-classical texts assume. As Hamlet might counter, 'ay, there's the rub!' for this could invite consideration of social power in the market, a prospect that may be unappealing to those who gain from current arrangements. Certain private interests are more likely to favour the rhetorical practice of perfectly competitive markets, for it implies that regulated markets and policy intervention are unnecessary, and somehow the market will sort itself out (Stiglitz, 2001: 524). In business schools and university economics departments much of this translates into the principles of economic neo-liberalism associated with the political right. The photo in Exhibit 8.1 was taken in a university business school at which one of the authors previously worked. It was unofficially known – fondly and with a degree of humour it may be added – as a hidden political message masquerading as directional instructions to help students locate where to hand in their assignments.

In sum, students' business school education on matters of work, employment and people management can be infused with assumptions that take for granted or legitimise the idea that employers should be left alone to get on with the 'art' of management. Unfettered by regulation and supplied with latest toolkits to generate employee performance, business leaders can deliver the best of all possible worlds – if only they are left alone to do it as their ideology prescribes.

Exhibit Box 8.1   Neo-liberal economic thought in a university business school. Source: Photo taken by one of the authors

▬▬▬ the growing prominence of inequality

The consequences of these assumptions are, however, problematic at a very practical level. In this regard we would invite you to consider the graphs below which show income inequality in the United States. For example, Image 8.2a (in Exhibit Box 8.2) illustrates that in 1978 the income-inequality gap was about eightfold: that is, the top income earners earned eight times the average worker's income. You might say that is unequal. Perhaps it is. But now compare that to 2010 (Image 8.2b), when the inequality gap soared to over 32:1. The pattern is comparable across other market economies such as the UK or Australia. Image 8.2c depicts a suspension bridge image: the peak years of 1928 and 2007 reveal that 1 per cent of top wage earners took home 23 per cent of the national income.

To appreciate what is occurring here, Thomas Piketty, in his widely acclaimed 2014 text *Capital in the Twenty First Century*, applying econometric analysis to large macro data shows how much free-market systems result in gross inequalities. In the 19th century, Western industrialising societies were highly unequal. Private wealth eclipsed national income and was concentrated in the hands of a small number of affluent elites, at the expense of a relatively impoverished minority. However, the trend of rising inequality was reversed between 1930 and 1975 due to a combination of factors: the Great Depression and a debt-fuelled recession destroyed much wealth. Policy considerations of the 1930s to address the problems prompted greater acceptability of state intervention in the economy with a programme of redistributing income, which expanded further after the Second World War. Capitalism became embedded in various rules and regulations that 'de-commodified' labour by providing social welfare and labour market support arrangements to redistributed national income: in America there was the New Deal and in Britain a social contract and Keynesian demand-led investments. Joint regulation between employers and workers through collective bargaining contributed to this process – the more than eight decades of reduced income inequality depicted in the suspension bridge graphic in Exhibit Box 8.2 – that is, until the great transformation post-1980 of the neo-liberal period discussed in Chapter 3.

For Piketty, the elites who sit at the top of the national income ladders have reasserted themselves in the neo-liberal period and a 'patrimonial capitalism', based upon inherited wealth and expanding inequality, has mushroomed since the mid-1980s. So market mechanisms are unlikely to correct this trend. Far from the textbook treatments of competitive markets with no actor holding undue market power, the elites' concentration of wealth enables them to rig the market in their favour. Unregulated markets reinforce a snowballing of wealth concentration and further the polarisation of incomes. If untouched, such trends will divide society between the 'haves' and 'have nots'. Political instability will ensue. The liberal democratic order may sink into decay

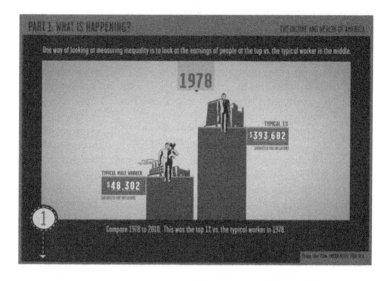

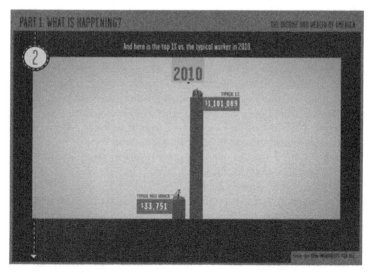

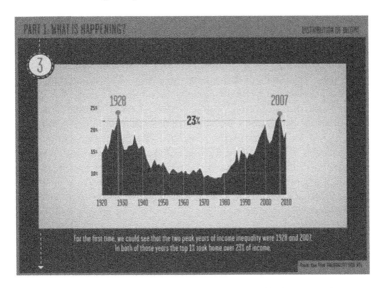

Exhibit Box 8.2   Income concentration in the US. Graphics from *Inequality for All.*

Credit: The Weinstein Company LLC (see: http://inequalityforall.com/resources/#).

or authoritarianism, as seems portended at the time of writing by phenomena such as 'Trumpism' in the United States. The social consequences of patrimonial capitalism, in a context of free movement of labour and deregulated markets, may well produce a nasty strain of nationalism and racism as the 'have nots', trapped in a brutish existence of squeezed living standards and imposed inequality, turn their ire on the easily identifiable 'outsiders' who become *the* source of all social ills (immigrants or welfare claimants). The current rise of the far right across Europe may well be one forewarning of a less palatable future. Indeed, in 2016, the desire for 'Brexit' in the UK was partly fuelled by the alienation and resentment of those social classes left behind in a post-industrial 'Sports Direct' Britain.

For many ER scholars, a positive contribution to avoid unequal outcomes is through greater social intervention into the market and more equitable redistribution of wealth. Such now is the prominence of inequality in society that it has become mainstream in much of our political discourse: the prominence of Bernie Sanders in the Democratic presidential nominee campaign in 2015 and 2016 is one indicator of how even in the heartlands of liberal-market America, members of the political class are amenable to discussing inequality. The British Prime Minister Theresa May, on taking office after the Brexit political melt-down, started talking of addressing inequality and improving indus-trial democracy by protecting those who are just managing to keep their jobs and struggling to pay their bills. This may potentially involve a counter-movement against the continued marketisation of society and sponsor re-regulation of the economy through the crea-tion of social protections, like labour laws and wealth taxes. Whether such a programme of reform is possible or desirable remains uncertain and is clearly a matter of political persuasion. Whatever argument one favours it is difficult to dismiss the notion that the employment rela-tionship, a central dynamic to the motor of wealth creation in society, is crucial to addressing these issues. As we have suggested above, and throughout this book at different times, the employment relationship is too important to be left as the preserve of employer prerogatives, whatever the assumptions of neo-classical economics or I&O psy-chologists might suggest. ER recognises a crucial divergence of inter-ests between the key actors in employment and identifies how the balance of power is structured. ER recognises that if left unchecked, unfettered employer power will likely lead to socially undesirable out-comes of which economic and social inequality is but one very important consequence.

automation, digital technology and inequality

Concerns around inequality also lie at the heart of current debates around new digital technology. Unless you have been hibernating up a mountain with no wi-fi or mobile signal for the last several years, we are all familiar with the pace of technological change and its impact on our lives. At least two of the authors can recall, as childhood fans, the long-running BBC programme *Tomorrow's World* (1965 to 2003). In addition to showing wacky inventions – such as the electric sounds used by the band Kraftwerk or a fold-up car that fitted into a suitcase – the presenters communicated a positive and upbeat message that future technologies would make work easier and life much more pleasant: we should all rejoice and expect to have an abundance of leisure time as technology becomes so advanced it will do our unwanted jobs for us. Similar arguments exist today, as digital technology is said to poten-tially empower individual workers by encouraging many to become their own bosses: like drivers using the Uber app or the millions of people earning a wage in the 'gig economy' by signing up as participants on the burgeoning crowdsourcing platforms, such as CrowdFlower or Amazon Mechanical Turk. Routine activities like paying for groceries in supermarkets or checking into a hotel are often automated. However, these technologies are not socially neutral, without implications for ongoing employment relationships. By way of example, one of the authors is a regular at a WH Smith in a UK airport. The visit usually entails the author stocking up on sufficient quantities of *Sherbet Dip* and *Curly-Wurly* chocolate bars prior to boarding. Most of the time, he has to regularly engage with the automated checkouts as there is rarely a member of staff servicing the manual tills. Over time, this exchange between man and machine has progressively evolved into a battle of wits. Pay with a ten pound note and you can be sure to receive a quantity of silver and copper coins for change that only Long John Silver would be proud of. If it is not a deluge of coinage, however, it's boarding pass requests that subsequently freeze the machine or repeated failures to read the barcode of items scanned. Granted the author is technologically incompetent, but at the same time his experience seems to be replicated by many other customers. Indeed queues reminiscent of a former Eastern bloc country are now common at the store as customers become entangled in the machine's clench, a process not helped by the fact that at least one of the three automated checkouts available is usually 'out of order'. On one occasion when the author was caught in the midst of a WH Smith 'tailback', his craving for sherbet momentarily receded and he began to reflect on his situation. Why had WH Smith's management made this decision? The customers do not seem to particularly enjoy the experience (indeed that campaigning tribune of social justice the *Daily Mail* started a campaign against automated checkouts in 2015). The author has observed how there is typically only one store assistant rostered who – at least when the author is there – spends most of her time helping customers use the allegedly 'self-service' checkouts. His observations concluded, and his purchase finally scanned and paid for, the author broached the assistant on her view of the machine before leaving. The response was negative: the machines are a nuisance, for they divert her time from keeping the shelves fully stocked, a practice which she gets randomly assessed on, and which contributes to the performance element of her pay. So for most of the shop assistant's day, she is trying to please frustrated customers who are almost always in a rush, while facing the pressures and stresses of meeting other managerial targets and demands. She has no voice, no say in the technology or its uses, and limited opportunities to change the consequences of automation on her job quality. One might wager that for WH Smith management on the other hand, there is the likely benefit of substantial cost savings presumably derived from the fact that they no longer have to pay the wages for additional shop assistants. So here perhaps is an action, undertaken by executives in pursuit of 'efficiencies', which have, in this context at least, unfavourable consequences for both staff and customers.

Personal experiences aside, contemporary debates about automation and digital technology also have darker overtones which have awakened old Luddite fears that employer adoption of robots and the like will erode job security, degrade the experience of work and exacerbate inequality. Such concerns are contentious, and indeed history tends to demonstrate that new technology creates as many new jobs as it destroys (Kochan, 2015).

Yet some of the concerns about technological unemployment may well be real. Carl Frey and Michael Osborne (2013) have concluded that 47 per cent of US jobs are at high risk from technological automation.[41] In the 19th century, they argue, machines replaced artisans and benefited unskilled labour. In the 20th century, computers replaced middle-income jobs, creating a polarised labour market. Over the next decade it seems probable that jobs in transportation, logistics, administration and a lot of what remains in manufacturing are at risk of displacement by automated processes. Moreover, computerisation will substitute for low-skill and low-wage jobs in the near future. By contrast, a reservoir of high-skill and high-wage occupations are the least susceptible to robotic or computer capital. Brynjolfsson and McAfee (2014), in their much reported *The Second Machine Age*, see the prospect of a 'winner-take-all' economy in which the income, wealth and life chances of a small number of highly skilled elite and computer capital owners soar ahead of the rest of society. The concept of 'digital Taylorism' echoes this sentiment (Brown et al., 2010). This argues that knowledge skills, once thought the route to prosperity in developed economies will face a similar fate to craft skills of the 19th century. Like the skilled crafts, contemporary knowledge workers increasingly experience jobs being broken down, de-skilled, codified and digitised. Where bank managers on the high street once used personal judgement to decide loan-worthy customers, computer software now dominates that task. The mass of employees, whether or not they hold high university qualifications, will find their future job reduced to routine functions commanding only modest wages.

Sometimes the debate around increased automation has had an unfortunate tendency to abstract technological change from the cut and thrust of employment relations (Spencer, 2016). There is an assumption that technological change 'just happens' and we all have to adapt as a result. But technology is heavily embedded in social relations between employer and employee in a workplace. To be sure, technological change can occur independently of the employment relationship.[42] Yet the origins of how, or if, technology is used in employment, as well as the outcomes that flow from its adoption, are not neutral. The dynamic is very much conditioned by the interests and power imbalances that exist in the employment relationship. We mentioned as much in previous chapters when we suggested that concerns about automation leading to mass unemployment may be hype: there is so much cheap labour about that many employers have little incentive to invest huge financial resources in risky new technology developments. It is also evident that employers may use the potential of new technologies to de-skill jobs or degrade and dehumanise employees' experience of work. Alternatively, employers may forego more efficient technologies if the consequences weigh too heavily on profit margins. Employers may simply opt to rely on sweating low-cost and disposable non-union labour. Similarly, the influence of financialisation, as we saw in Chapter 3, may retard employers from investing if the returns are uncertain or deemed too risky. Finally, a less obvious reason that may check employers' willingness to displace people's jobs with robots and forego the acclaimed efficiency-generating potential relates to issues of power and control in the workplace. Although it seems feasible that many office workers could exploit the benefits of things like cloud computing by working digitally from home, or virtually anywhere in the world, a significant bulk of managers opt to subject their staff to the observed controllable confines of the workplace under the watchful gaze of the supervisor or team leader. Indeed, one suspects that was part of the motivation behind the much reported case of Yahoo reversing its policy of supporting home working amongst its employees in the US.[43]

conclusion

It is at this point that we conclude not just this chapter but the book. We hope this chapter, along with the others found within these pages, has demonstrated the relevance and vitality of ER as a field of study when engaging with the topic of work and employment. An awareness of the employment relationship and its underlying dynamics of power and interests has found particular resonance in this chapter and the book. Much of the analysis of employment and labour markets which curries favour in the mainstream curricula of ubiquitous business school modules – like the fields of OB and neo-classical economics discussed here – has potential to elide some important questions around the wider political contours of society and the structure of organisations. The study of ER, in contrast, can direct us to the enduring tendencies towards conflict and cooperation, the diversity of actors' interests and how these are accommodated, mediated and reconciled (or, in some cases, suppressed) alongside the wider societal context in which employment exchanges are embedded. This enables us to see how technology in the workplace, for example, is far from neutral but is intimately entwined in the nature of the power exchange between employer and worker. Some of our passages have been purposely light-hearted and we have had our fun critiquing human resource managers, economists, and, not to forget Mr Kunz or Ken Dodd and his Diddymen. Yet behind the comedy and popular culture, we hope, is a serious message. In these times when so many of our problems appear tractable to the growing inequalities of contemporary economics, we believe that the study of employment relations, its actors, context, processes and outcomes, reveals many of the underlying sources of our present day social ills and the way organisations shape our lives.

We have seen how the big issues of our day – austerity, financialisation, workplace relationships, conflict, participation, low pay, long hours and digital technology – are all deeply connected to the study of work and employment in all its various forms. As a field of study ER is rich, dynamic and exciting. It can, as we have shown, make a call for the better management of people at work, and help support a more informed individual (student) who can question the rhetorical claims of prescriptive best practice models. So while the employment relationship may be embedded in various constraints and ongoing tensions, there can be policy choices that aim to support a fairer and more equitable workplace while seeking to meet efficiency demands. As we have pointed out in Chapters 3 and 4, no one would prefer to be employed under insecurity, austerity or a badly managed firm. A study of employment relations helps us appreciate how organisations can meet the various competing demands of different actors and institutions to produce better outcomes for all, not just for one vested or corporate group. As Kochan (2015: xi) has suggested, 'we are not just pawns controlled by globalisation, technological changes, or any other force totally out of our control. If we take the right actions and work together, we can shape the future of work in ways that work for all.' Indeed, the work of ER scholars has for decades positively engaged with and shaped government policy and organisational practice aimed at improving employee wellbeing, social justice and economic equality.[44] On that basis we hope you will agree that it is vital that the study of ER should continue to grow and flourish by offering critical insight and that this book in its own very short, fairly interesting and reasonably cheap way, has sparked your interest to engage further with the subject and perhaps contribute ideas for more equitable changes about the future of work relationships.

Notes

1   'Vicars are employed by God, not the Church', says Court in land-mark ruling', *The Independent*, 30 April 2015

2   'China saw a dramatic increase in wage arrears protests in run up to New Year,' *China Labour Bulletin*, 2 March 2016

3   'The risk of the wage-work bargain', The *Unpaid Britain* Project, 24 March 2016

4   'London 2012 staff still waiting to be paid', *BBC Inside Out*, 22 February 2016

5   Such housing estates are now exclusive and extremely expensive suburbs in which to live in Britain, now listed as protected heritage buildings: for example, Port Sunlight on the Wirral in Merseyside, or Bourneville Village in Birmingham, built for the workers of Unilever (Port Sunlight) and Cadbury (Bourneville).

6   Incidentally, this is a very fine tactic to improve your country's chances of doing well in international football. From such recruit-ment strategies the French indirectly got Zinedine Zidane, the Swedes Zlatan Ibrahimović, the Germans Mesut Özil, while the English got Wayne Rooney.

7   'Why robots are coming for US service jobs', *Financial Times*, 3 May 2016; 'Meet the cobots: humans and robots together on the factory floor', *Financial Times*, 5 May 2016

8   'The great American bubble machine', *Rolling Stone*, 9–23 July 2009

9   Denning, S. (2014) 'Why IBM is in decline', *Forbes Online*, 3 May

10 'Laid off IBM employee says the company is blowing it by cutting the wrong people', *Business Insider*, 18 April 2012

11 One might note it is never clear or defined at which point a busi-ness achieves 'maximisation'. The quest for continuous (maximum) returns typically means squeezing costs from other stakeholders (including employees).

12 Of course not all shareholders are disinterested, cold calculators of financial return. Even in *Wall Street*, Gordon Gekko's rival, the investor Sir Lawrence Wildman, wants to take over and modernise a steel company to modernise and save '*lives and jobs, three and four generations of steelworkers*'. Then again, Gekko did claim he was doing similar with the planned airline acquisition.

13 Mayer, C. (2013) 'Leadership: What's lost when shareholders rule', *Harvard Business Review Online*, 13 May

14 An interesting side note to all this is that Peter Hartz would later be convicted by the German courts for imbursing the former head of the Volkswagen Works Council special payments of close to €2 million to secure favourable votes in important company decisions. The Volkswagen HR department were also found to have organised lavish trips abroad for members of the works council, which even involved flying over favoured Brazilian prostitutes (see 'VW boss says he did not know of perks and prostitutes', *The Guardian*, 10 January 2008). Even for scholars who admire the German 'cooperative' works council system, such activities give added meaning to the notion of 'consensual industrial relations'.

15 'Does David Cameron's taste in films match his values? If...only', *The Guardian*, 6 January 2012

16 'South African police shoot dead striking miners', *The Guardian*, 17 August 2012

17 'The march of the robots into Chinese factories', *Bloomberg Businessweek*, 30 November 2012

18 'No end to the assassinations in Colombia', *International Trade Union Confederation*, 29 June 2009

19 Although note that what 'stability' actually means, and in whose interests, can be a contentious issue.

20 Space precludes a full discussion of the emergence of 'new actors' on the ER scene; however, we note that there are other civil society organisations (CSO) that attract scholarly interest in this regard, such as Citizens Advice or Stonewall (in the UK). These and other similar advocacy agencies represent particular issues in society (e.g. age, gender, disability, lesbian rights) which can overlap into employee concerns, perhaps because of union membership decline over recent decades. See Heery et al. (2014) for a discussion of the representative role of CSOs in ER.

21 For a very literal illustration of the consequences of what can happen when work access is denied on a large scale, check out the *World in Action* documentary of the same name available online. You might want search YouTube for the example.

22 See, for example, 'Death toll among Qatar's 2022 World Cup workers revealed', *The Guardian*, 23 December 2014 or 'Hundreds of Nepalis die on World Cup infrastructure projects in Qatar', *The Telegraph*, 24 January, 2014.

23 For some light amusement search YouTube for some classic *Coronation Street* episodes depicting contemporary ER issues: 'Trouble at Mike Baldwin's factory' or 'Factory girls on strike at Coronation Street factory'.

24   'Gervinho demanded a private beach and helicopter as former Arsenal striker's move to Abu Dhabi side Al Jazira collapses', *Independent*, 30 June 2015

25   'Apple and Facebook offer to freeze eggs for female employees', *The Guardian*, 15 October 2014

26   'Google your way to a wacky office', *BBC News*, 13 March 2008

27   For interest, view the clip on YouTube: www.youtube.com/watch?v=M3-s72NToTw

28   'Company may face action over "family profiling"', *Irish Independent*, 29 November 2006

29   Data from Health and Safety Executive (HSE), www.hse.gov.uk/statistics/dayslost.htm and Trades Union Congress (TUC), www.tuc.org.uk/government-threat-safety-reps

30   The worker director idea was suggested at time of writing by Theresa May in her opening speech as new British Prime Minister after the Brexit vote in the UK (see Gall, 2016).

31   Source: www.whitehouse.gov/the-press-office/2015/10/07/remarks-president-white-house-summit-worker-voice

32   Source: www.whitehouse.gov/the-press-office/2015/10/07/remarks-president-white-house-summit-worker-voice

33   '"Because Marissa said so" – Yahoos bristle at Mayer's QPR ranking system and "silent layoffs"', *Wall Street Journal*, 8 November 2013

34   'B&Q offers to negotiate compensation for changes to staff benefits,' *The Guardian*, 12 April 2016

35   'Church of England pays some workers below living wage', *BBC News*, 23 February 2015

36   'Workers contribute £32bn to UK economy from unpaid overtime', TUC Online, 27 February 2015

37   'The employees shut inside coffins', *BBC Magazine*, 14 December 2015, www.bbc.co.uk/news/magazine-34797017

38   Taylor, L. 'THE Comment', *Times Higher Education*, 23 June 2016.

39   In sociology and economics, 'immiseration' refers to classical Marxist theory about the material deprivation and diminishing conditions of the working classes as capitalism continues to expand and develop over time. The principle is applied here to a possible equally impoverished educational experience across mainstream (uncritical, prescriptive) business school learning.

40   Gall, G. 'The death of industrial relations', *The Guardian*, 28 January 2008

41   Frey and Osborne's data, on a more positive note at least, thankfully predicts that accountants will become a thing of the past by 2033.

42 Indeed, most technological innovation is developed through state initiatives and public spending into research and development (Mazzucato, 2011).
43 'Yahoo chief bans homeworking', *The Guardian*, 25 February 2013
44 Greer (2011: 405) comments how ER academics are known for their level of engagement and activity: speaking on the media, supporting public meetings, and several have honours from the Queen for their activity.

References

Ackers, P. (2007) 'Collective bargaining as industrial democracy: Hugh Clegg and the political foundations of British industrial relations pluralism', *British Journal of Industrial Relations*, 45(1): 77–101.

Ackers, P. (2015) 'Trade unions as professional associations', in S. Johnstone and P. Ackers (eds) *Finding a Voice at Work? New Perspectives in Employment Relations*. Oxford: Oxford University Press.

Akerlof, G. and Yellen, J. (1990) 'The fair wage effort hypothesis and unemployment', *Quarterly Journal of Economics*, 97(4): 543–69.

Armstrong, P., Glyn, A. and Harrison, J. (1991) *Capitalism since World War 2*. Oxford: Blackwell.

Atzeni, M. (2016) 'Capitalism, workers organising and the shifting meanings of workplace democracy', *Labor History*, 57(3): 374–89.

Baccaro, L. and Howell, C. (2011) 'A common neoliberal trajectory: the transformation of industrial relations in advanced capitalism', *Politics and Society*, 39(4): 521–63.

Barrow, C. (1993) *Critical Theories of the State: Marxist, Neo-Marxist, Post-Marxist*. Madison, WI: University of Wisconsin Press.

Barry, M. and Wilkinson, A. (2016) 'Pro-social or pro-management? A critique of employee voice as pro-social behaviour within organisational behaviour', *British Journal of Industrial Relations*, 54(2): 261–84.

Batstone, E., Boraston, I. and Frenkel, S. (1978) *The Social Organization of Strikes*. Oxford: Basil Blackwell.

Batt, R.L. and Appelbaum, E. (2013) 'The impact of financialization on management and employment outcomes', Upjohn Institute Working Paper, No. 13-191. Kalamazoo, MI: W.E. Upjohn Institute for Employment Research.

Bellamy-Foster, J. and Magdoff, F. (2009) *The Great Financial Crisis: Causes and Consequences*. New York: Monthly Review Press.

Bellamy-Foster, J. and McChesney, R.W. (2012) *Endless Crisis: How Monopoly-Finance Capital Produces Stagnation and Upheaval from the USA to China*. New York: Monthly Review Press.

Berggren, C. (1992) *Alternatives to Lean Production*, Ithaca, NY: ILR Press.

Biggs, J. (2015) *All Day Long: A Portrait of Britain*. London: Serpent's Tail.

Blyth, M. (2015) *Austerity: The History of a Dangerous Idea*. Oxford: Oxford University Press.

Braverman, H. (1974) *Labor and Monopoly Capitalism: The Degradation of Work in the Twentieth Century*. New York: Monthly Review.

Brennan, D. (2015) *Life Interrupted: Trafficking into Forced Labour in the United States*. Durham: Duke University Press.

Brown, G.F. (1977) *Sabotage: A Study in Industrial Conflict*. Nottingham: Spokesman Books.

Brown, P., Lauder, H. and Ashton, D. (2010) *The Global Auction: The Broken Promises of Education, Jobs, and Incomes*. Oxford: Oxford University Press.

Brueggemann, J. (2000) 'The power and collapse of paternalism: the Ford Motor Company and black workers, 1937-1941', *Social Problems*, 47(2): 220–40.

Brynjolfsson, E. and McAfee, A. (2014) *The Second Machine Age: Work, Progress and Prosperity in a Time of Brilliant Technologies*. New York: W.W. Norton.

Budd, J. (2004) *Employment with a Human Face: Balancing Efficiency, Equity and Voice*. Ithaca: Cornell University Press.

Chang, H.J. (2014) *Economics: The User's Guide*. London: Pelican Books.

Cohen, G.A. (1983) 'The structure of proletarian unfreedom', *Philosophy and Public Affairs*, 12(1): 3–33.

Cowling, K. (1982) *Monopoly Capitalism*. London: Wiley.

Crouch, C. (1982) *Trade Unions: The Logic of Collective Action*. Glasgow: Fontana.

Crouch, C. (1993) *Industrial Relations and European State Traditions*. Oxford: Clarendon Press.

Crouch, C. (2009) 'Privatized Keynesianism: an unacknowledged policy regime', *British Journal of Politics and International Relations*, 11(3): 382–99.

Cushen, J. and Thompson, P. (2012) 'Doing the right thing? HRM and the angry knowledge worker', *New Technology, Work and Employment*, 27(2): 79–92.

Cushen, J. and Thompson, P. (2016) 'Financialization and value: why labour and the labour process still matter', *Work, Employment and Society*, 30(2): 352–65.

Darlington, R. and Lyddon, R. (2001) *Glorious Summer: Class Struggle in Britain, 1972*. London: Bookmarks.

Dobbins, A., Plows, A. and Lloyd-Williams, H. (2014) '"Make do and mend" after redundancy at Anglesey Aluminium: critiquing human capital approaches to unemployment', *Work, Employment and Society*, 28(4): 515–32.

Doellgast, V. (2008) 'Collective bargaining and high-involvement management in comparative perspective: evidence from U.S. and German call centers', *Industrial Relations: A Journal of Economy and Society*, 47(2): 284–319.

Donaghey, J., Cullinane, N., Dundon, T. and Wilkinson, A. (2011) 'Reconceptualising employee silence: problems and prognosis', *Work, Employment and Society*, 25(1): 56–67.

Dundon, T. (2014) 'So what is the value of that expensive MBA?', *Irish Times*, 6 May. Available at: www.irishtimes.com/news/education/so-what-is-the-value-of-that-expensive-mba-1.1781547, accessed on 10 February 2016.

Dundon, T. and Rollinson, D. (2011) *Understanding Employment Relations*, 2nd edition. London: McGraw-Hill.

Dundon, T. and Wilkinson, A. (2017) 'Employee involvement and participation', in A. Wilkinson, T. Redman and T. Dundon (eds) *Contemporary HRM: Texts and Cases*, 5e. Harlow: Pearson.

Edwards, P.K. (1986) *Conflict at Work*. Oxford: Blackwell.

Edwards, P.K. (2003) 'The employment relationship and the field of industrial relations', in P.K. Edwards (ed.) *Industrial Relations: Theory and Practice*, 2nd edition. Oxford: Blackwell.

Felstead, A., Gallie, D., Green, F. and Inanc, H. (2014) Skills and employment survey 2012. Available at: https://discover.ukdataservice.ac.uk/catalogue/?sn=7466&type=data%20catalogue, accessed on 9 October 2016.

Fox, A. (1966) 'Managerial ideology and labour relations', *British Journal of Industrial Relations*, 4(1): 366–78.

Fox, A. (1985) *Man Mismanagement*, 2nd edition. London: Hutchinson.

Frege, C. (2007) *Employment Research and State Traditions: A Comparative History of Britain, Germany and the United States*. Oxford: Oxford University Press.

French, J.R.P. and Raven, B.H. (1959), 'The bases of social power', in D. Cartwright (ed.), *Studies in Social Power*. Ann Arbor, MI: University of Michigan.

Frey, C.B. and Osborne, M.A. (2013) *The Future of Employment: How Susceptible Are Jobs to Computerisation*. Oxford Martin School, University of Oxford. Available at: www.oxfordmartin.ox.ac.uk/publications/view/1314, accessed on 12 April 2016.

Gall, G. (2008) 'The death of industrial relations', *The Guardian*, 28 January.

Gall, G. (2016) 'Theresa May, prime minister: the ball is in her court on workplace democracy. *The Conversation*, 13 July. Available at: https://theconversation.com/theresa-may-prime-minister-the-ball-is-in-her-court-on-workplace-democracy-62388, accessed on 15 July 2016.

Gaskell, E. (1998) *North and South*. Ware, Hertfordshire: Wordsworth (originally published in 1855).

Geary, R. (1985) *Policing Industrial Disputes, 1893–1985*. Cambridge: Cambridge University Press.

Glyn, A. (2007) *Capitalism Unleashed: Finance, Globalisation and Welfare*. Oxford: Oxford University Press.

Godard, J. (2014) 'The psychologisation of employment relations?', *Human Resource Management Journal*, 24(1): 1–18.

Graeber, D. (2013) 'On the phenomenon of bullshit jobs', *Strike! Magazine*, 17 August. Available at: http://strikemag.org/bullshit-jobs

Greenberg, J. (1990) 'Employee theft as a reaction to underpayment or inequity: the hidden cost of pay cuts', *Journal of Applied Psychology*, 75(5): 561–568.

Greene, A.M. (2003) 'Women and industrial relations', in P. Ackers and A. Wilkinson (eds) *Understanding Work and Employment: Industrial Relations in Transition*. Oxford: Oxford University Press.

Greer, I. (2011) 'Book Review: What's the Point of Industrial Relations? In Defence of Critical Social Science', *British Journal of Industrial Relations*, 49(2): 404–6.

Grey, C. (2005) *A Very Short, Reasonably Interesting and Reasonably Cheap Book about Studying Organizations*. London: Sage.

Grey, C. (2009) *A Very Short, Reasonably Interesting and Reasonably Cheap Book about Studying Organizations*, 2e. London: Sage.

Grimshaw, D. and Rubery, J. (2008) 'Economics and HRM', in P. Boxall, J. Purcell and P.M. Wright (eds) *Oxford Handbook of Human Resource Management*. Oxford: Oxford University Press.

Hahnel, R. (2015) *The ABCs of Political Economy: A Modern Approach*. London: Pluto Press.

Haldane, A. (2015) 'Drag and drop'. Speech to BizClub Lunch, Rutland, 19 March. Available at: www.bankofengland.co.uk/publications/Pages/speeches/2015/810.aspx

Hall, P. and Soskice, D. (eds) (2001) *Varieties of Capitalism: The Institutional Foundations of Comparative Advantage*. Oxford: Oxford University Press.

Hancké, B., Rhodes, M. and Thatcher, M. (eds) (2007) *Beyond Varieties of Capitalism: Conflict, Contradictions, and Complementarities in the European Economy*. Oxford: Oxford University Press.

Harley, B., Sargent, L. and Allen, B. (2010) 'Employee responses to "high performance work system" practices: an empirical test of the disciplined worker thesis', *Work, Employment and Society*, 24(4): 740-60.

Harvey, D. (2007) *A Brief History of Neoliberalism*. Oxford: Oxford University Press.

Harvey, D. (2011) *The Enigma of Capital and the Crises of Capitalism*. London: Profile Books.

Heery, E. (2015) 'Frames of reference and worker participation', in S. Johnstone and P. Ackers (eds) *Finding a Voice at Work? New Perspectives in Employment Relations*. Oxford: Oxford University Press.

Heery, E., Abbott, B. and Williams, S. (2014) 'Civil society organisations and employee voice', in A. Wilkinson, J. Donaghy, T. Dundon and R. Freeman (eds) *Handbook of Research on Employee Voice*. Cheltenham: Edward Elgar.

Herman, E.S. and Chomsky, N. (1988) *Manufacturing Consent: The Political Economy of the Mass Media*. New York: Pantheon Books.

Herod, A., Rainnie, A. and McGrath-Champ, S. (2007) 'Working space: why incorporating the geographical is central to theorizing work and employment practices', *Work, Employment and Society*, 21(2): 247–64.

Heyes, J., Lewis, P. and Clark, I. (2014) 'Varieties of capitalism reconsidered: learning from the Great Recession and its aftermath', in M. Hauptmeier and M. Vidal (eds) *Comparative Political Economy at Work*. Basingstoke: Palgrave Macmillan.

Hill, R. and Myatt, T. (2010) *The Economics Anti-Textbook: A Critical Thinker's Guide to Microeconomics*. Black Point, Nova Scotia: Fernwood Publishing.

Howell, C. (2007) *Trade Unions and the State: The Construction of Industrial Relations Institutions in Britain, 1890–2000*. New Jersey: Princeton University Press.

Hudson, M. (2015) *Killing the Host: How Financial Parasites and Debt Destroy the Global Economy*. New York: Perseus Books.

Hyman, R. (1984) *Strikes*. London: Fontana.

Hyman, R. (2015) 'The very idea of democracy at work', *Transfer: European Review of Labour and Research*, 22 (1): 11–24.

Jacobs, K., Perry, I. and MacGillvary, J. (2015) *The High Public Cost of Low Wages*, UC Berkeley Labor Center. Available at: http://laborcenter.berkeley.edu/pdf/2015/the-high-public-cost-of-low-wages.pdf

Jessop, B. (1990) *State Theory: Putting the Capitalist State in Its Place*. Cambridge: Polity Press.

Johnstone, S. and Wilkinson, A. (eds) (2016) *Developing Positive Employment Relations*. Basingstoke: Palgrave.

Joseph Rowntree Foundation (2015) *In-work Poverty Levels*, 23 November. Available at: www.jrf.org.uk/data/work-poverty-levels, accessed on 10 December 2015.

Juravich, T. (1988) *Chaos on the Shop Floor: A Worker's View of Productivity, Quality and Management*. Philadelphia: Temple University Press.

Kahn-Freund, O. (1972) *Labour and the Law*. London: Stevens and Sons.

Kalecki, M. (1943) 'Political aspects of full employment', *The Political Quarterly*, 14(4): 322–30.

Kantor, J. and Streitfeld, D. (2015) 'Inside Amazon: wrestling big ideas in a bruising workplace', *New York Times*, 15 August. Available at: www.nytimes.com/2015/08/16/technology/inside-amazon-wrestling-big-ideas-in-a-bruising-workplace.html?_r=0

Katz, H. (1985) *Shifting Gears: Changing Labor Relations in the U.S. Automobile Industry*. Cambridge, MA: MIT Press.

Kaufman, B. (2007) 'An institutional economic analysis of labor unions', *Industrial Relations*, 51(1): 438–71.

Kelly, J. (2004) 'Social partnership agreements in Britain: Labor cooperation and compliance', *Industrial Relations: A Journal of Economy and Society*, 43(1): 267–92.

Kochan, T.A. (2015) *Shaping the Future of Work: What Future Worker, Business, Government, and Education Leaders Need to Do for All to Prosper*. New York: Business Expert Press.

Koller, F. (2010) *Spark: How Old Fashioned Values Drive a Twenty-First Century Corporation*. New York: Public Affairs.

Korpi, W. (1983) *The Democratic Class Struggle*. London: Routledge.

Koukiadaki, A., Távora, I. and Martínez-Lucio, M. (eds) (2016) *Joint Regulation and Labour Market Policy in Europe during the Crisis*. Brussels: European Trade Union Institute (ETUI). Available at: www.etui.org/Publications2/Books/Joint-regulation-and-labour-market-policy-in-Europe-during-the-crisis, accessed on 12 July 2016.

Lapavitsas, C. (2012a) *Crisis in the Eurozone*. London: Verso Books.

Lapavitsas, C. (2012b) 'Introduction: a crisis of financialisation', in C. Lapavitsas (ed.) *Financialisation in Crisis*. Leiden, The Netherlands: Brill.

Lapavitsas, C. (2013) *Profiting without Producing: How Finance Exploits Us All*. London: Verso.

Lukes, S. (2005) *Power: A Radical View*, Revised 2nd edition. Basingstoke: Palgrave Macmillan.

Mabey, C. and Mayrhofer, W. (2015) (eds) *Developing Leadership: Questions Business Schools Don't Ask*. London: Sage.

MacInnes, T., Tinson, A., Hughes, C., Born, T.B. and Aldridge, H. (2015) *Monitoring Poverty and Social Exclusion*, Annual Report. York: Joseph Rowntree Foundation. Available at: www.jrf.org.uk/mpse-2015

Mankiw, G. (2015) *Principles of Economics*, 7th edition. Stamford, CT: South Western College Publishing, Cengage Learning.

Manning, A. (2005) *Monopsony in Motion: Imperfect Competition in Labor Markets*. Princeton, NJ: Princeton University Press.

Manning, A. (2015) 'Shifting the balance of power: workers, employers and wages over the next parliament', in G. Kelly and C. D'Arcy (eds) *Securing a Pay Rise: The Path Back to Shared Wage Growth*. London: Resolution Foundation.

Marchington, M. and Wilkinson, A. (2012) *Human Resource Management at Work: People Management and Development*, 5th edition. London: CIPD Publishing.

Marchington, M., Goodman, J., Wilkinson, A. and Ackers, P. (1992) *New Developments in Employee Involvement*. Research Paper No. 2. London: Department of Employment.

Mars, G. (1982) *Cheats at Work: An Anthropology of Workplace Crime*. London: Allen and Unwin.

Marsden, D. (1999) *The Theory of Employment Systems: Micro-foundations of Societal Diversity*. Oxford: Oxford University Press.

Martin, R. (1992) *Bargaining Power*. Oxford: Clarendon Press.

Marx, K. (1992) *Capital: Volume 1: A Critique of Political Economy*. London: Penguin Classics (originally published in 1867).

Mayer, C. (2013) 'Leadership: What's lost when shareholders rule', *Harvard Business Review Online*, 13 May.

Mazzucato, M. (2011) *The Entrepreneurial State: Debunking Public vs Private Myths*. London: Anthem Press.

McDonough, T. and Dundon, T. (2010) 'Thatcherism delayed? The Irish crisis and the paradox of social partnership', *Industrial Relations Journal*, 41(6): 544–62.

Meixell, B. and Eisenberry, R. (2014) *An Epidemic of Wage Theft Is Costing Workers Hundreds of Millions of Dollars a Year*. Washington, DC: Economic Policy Institute. Available at: www.epi.org/files/2014/wage-theft.pdf

Migration Advisory Committee (2014) *Migrants in Low-skilled Work: The Growth of EU and Non-EU Labour in Low-skilled Jobs and Its Impact on the UK*. London: Home Office.

Mirowski, P. (2014) *Never Let a Serious Crisis Go to Waste: How Neoliberalism Survived the Financial Meltdown*. London: Verso.

Mitlacher, L.W. (2007) 'The role of temporary agency work in different industrial relations systems: a comparison between Germany and the USA', *British Journal of Industrial Relations*, 45(3): 581–606.

Nichols, T. and Beynon, H. (1977) *Living With Capitalism*. London: Routledge and Kegan Paul.

Noble, D. (2000) 'Social choice in machine design: the case of automatically controlled machine tools', in D. Preece, I. McLoughlin and P. Dawson (eds) *Technology, Organizations and Innovation: Critical Perspectives on Business and Management, Volume 1: The Early Debates*. London: Routledge.

OECD (2015) *In It Together: Why Less Inequality Benefits Us All.* Paris: OECD Publishing.

Offe, C. and Wiesenthal, H. (1980) 'Two logics of collective action: theoretical notes on social class and organizational form', *Political Power and Social Theory*, 1: 67–115.

O'Sullivan, M., Turner, T., McMahon, J., Ryan, L., Lavelle, J., Murphy, C., O'Brien, M and Gunnigle, P. (2015) A Study on the Prevalence of Zero Hours Contracts among Irish Employers and their Impact on Employees. Dublin: Department of Jobs, Enterprise and Innovation. Available online: https://www.djei.ie/en/Publications/Publication-files/Study-on-the-Prevalence-of-Zero-Hours-Contracts.pdf (accessed 8 February 2017).

Parker, S. (ed.) (2013) *The Squeezed Middle: The Pressure on Ordinary Workers in America and Britain*. Chicago: Chicago University Press.

Peak, S. (1984) *Troops in Strikes: Military Intervention in Industrial Disputes*. London: Cobden Trust.

Pfeffer, J. (1998) *The Human Equation: Building Profits by Putting People First*. Boston, MA: Harvard Business Press.

Piketty, T. (2014) *Capital in the Twenty-First Century*. Cambridge, MA: Harvard University Press.

Pollard, S. (1963) 'Factory discipline in the Industrial Revolution', *Economic History Review*, 16(2): 254–71.

Pollert, A. (2005) 'The unorganised worker: the decline in collectivism and new hurdles to individual employment rights', *Industrial Law Journal*, 34(3): 217–38.

Purcell, J. (1987) 'Mapping management styles in employee relations', *Journal of Management Studies*, 24(5): 533–48.

Purcell, J. (2014) 'Disengaging from engagement', *Human Resource Management Journal*, 24(3): 241–54.

Purdy, D. (1988) *Social Power and the Labour Market: A Radical Approach to Labour Economics*. Basingstoke: Palgrave Macmillan.

Putnam, R.D. (2001) *Bowling Alone: The Collapse and Revival of American Community*. New York: Simon and Schuster.

Ramalho, J.R. and Francisco, E.M.V. (2008) 'Labour relations in the modular system: ten years of the VW experience at Resende, Brazil', in P. Stewart and V. Pulignano (eds) *Flexibility at Work: Critical Developments in the International Automobile Industry*. Basingstoke: Palgrave Macmillan.

Reich, R. (2003) *Inequality for All*. Documentary and website by Radius TWC, Los Angeles, California. Available at: http://inequality forall.com

Riddell, P. (1983) *The Thatcher Government*. Oxford: Martin Robertson.

Roscoe, P. (2014) *I Spend, Therefore I Am: The True Cost of Economics*. New York: Viking Press.

Rose, M. (1978) *Industrial Behaviour: Theoretical Developments since Taylor*. Harmondsworth: Penguin.

Routh, G. (1989) *The Origin of Economic Ideas*. London: Macmillan.

Royle, T. (2000) *Working for McDonald's*. London: Routledge.

Rubery, J. (2015) 'Change at work: feminization, flexibilisation, fragmentation and financialisation', *Employees Relations*, 37(6): 633–44.

Rubery, J. and Grimshaw, D. (2003) *The Organisation of Employment: An International Perspective*. London: Palgrave.

Rubery, J. and Rafferty, A. (2013) 'Women and recession revisited', *Work, Employment and Society*, 27(3): 414–32.

Rubinstein, S.A. and Kochan, T.A. (2001) *Learning from Saturn: Possibilities for Corporate Governance and Employee Relations*. Ithaca, NY: ILR Press.

Sayer, A. (2014) *Why We Can't Afford the Rich*. Bristol: Policy Press.

Schmidt, G. and Williams, K. (2002) 'German management facing globalization: the 'German Model' on trial', in M. Geppert, D. Matten and K. Williams (eds) *Challenges for European Management in a Global Context: Experiences from Britain and Germany*. Basingstoke: Palgrave Macmillan.

Seifert, R. (2015) 'Big bangs and cold wars: the British industrial relations tradition after Donovan, 1965–2015', *Employee Relations*, 37(6): 746–60.

Sisson, K. (2010) *Employment Relations Matter*. Available at: www2. warwick.ac.uk/fac/soc/wbs/research/irru/erm

Sissons, P. (2011) *The Hourglass and the Escalator: Labour Market Change and Mobility*. London: The Work Foundation.

Smith, C. (2006) 'The double indeterminacy of labour power', *Work, Employment and Society*, 20(2): 389–402.

Solzhenitsyn, A. (1962) *One Day in the Life of Ivan Denisovich*. New York: Bantam Books.

Spencer, D.A. (2009) *The Political Economy of Work*. London: Routledge.

Spencer, DA. (2016) 'Work in and beyond the Second Machine Age: the politics of production and digital technologies', *Work, Employment and Society*, Online Early: 1–11. DOI: 10.1177/0950017016645716.

Stiglitz, J. (2001) Information and Change in the Paradigm in Economics, Nobel Prize Lecture, 8 December. Available at: www.

nobelprize.org/nobel_prizes/economic-sciences/laureates/2001/stiglitz-lecture.html, accessed on 17 March 2016.

Stockhammer, E. (2012) 'Neo-liberalism, income distribution and the causes of the crisis' in P. Arestis, R. Sobreira and J.L. Oreiro (eds) *The Financial Crisis: Origins and Implications*. London: Springer.

Streeck, W. (1997) 'Beneficial constraints: on the economic limits of rational voluntarism', in J.R. Hollingsworth and R. Boyer (eds) *Contemporary Capitalism: The Embeddedness of Institutions*. Cambridge: Cambridge University Press.

Swenson, P. (1992) 'Union politics, the welfare state and intraclass conflict in Sweden and Germany', in M. Golden and J. Pontusson (eds) *Bargaining for Change: Union Politics in North America and Europe*. Ithaca, NY: Cornell University Press.

Taylor, L. (2016) 'THE Comment', *Times Higher Education*, 23 June.

Thompson, P. (2003) 'Disconnected capitalism: or why employers can't keep their side of the bargain', *Work, Employment and Society*, 17(2): 359–78.

Thompson, P. (2010) 'The capitalist labour process: concepts and connections', *Capital and Class*, 34(1): 7–14.

Thompson, P. and McHugh, D. (2009) *Work Organisations*, 4th edition. New York: Palgrave.

Traxler, F. (1998) 'Austria: still the country of corporatism?', in A. Ferner and R. Hyman (eds) *Changing Industrial Relations in Europe*, 2nd edition. Oxford: Wiley-Blackwell.

Traxler, F. (2003) 'Bargaining (de)centralization, macroeconomic performance and control over the employment relationship', *British Journal of Industrial Relations*, 41(1): 1–27.

Ulrich, D. (1998) 'A new mandate for human resources', *Harvard Business Review*, January–February, 125–34.

Upchurch, M., Taylor, G. And Mathers, A. (2009) *The Crisis of Social Democratic Trade Unionism in West Europe: The Search for Alternatives*. Abingdon: Ashgate Publishing.

Visser, J. (2010) 'The Crisis of Social Democratic Trade Unionism in Western Europe – The Search for Alternatives – by Martin Upchurch, Graham Taylor and Andrew Mathers', Book review, *British Journal of Industrial Relations*, 48(4): 813–15.

Wajcman, J. (2000) 'Feminism facing industrial relations in Britain', *British Journal of Industrial Relations*, 38(2): 183–201.

Western, B. and Rosenfeld, J. (2011) 'Unions, norms, and the rise in U.S. wage inequality', *American Sociological Review*, 78(4): 513–37.

Wilkinson A (2015) 'Employee voice', in A. Wilkinson and S. Johnstone (eds) *An Encyclopaedia of Human Resource Management*. Cheltenham: Edward Elgar.

Wilkinson A. (2016) Who is listening to employee voice? Keynote address – Innovation Arabia 9 Congress, Dubai, UAE.

Wilkinson, A., Donaghey, J., Dundon, T. and Freeman, R. (2014) (eds) *Handbook of Research on Employee Voice*. Cheltenham: Edward Elgar.

Wilkinson, A., Redman, T. and Dundon, T. (2017) *Contemporary Human Resource Management: Texts and Cases*, 5th edition. Harlow: Pearson Education.

Wilkinson, R. and Pickett, K. (2009) *The Spirit Level: Why More Equal Societies Almost Always Do Better*. London: Allen Lane.

Willman, P. (2017) 'Economics and Employment Relations', in A. Wilkinson, T. Dundon, J. Donaghey and A. Colvin (eds) *The Routledge Companion to Employment Relations*. London: Routledge.

Wolff, R.D. (2012) *Democracy at Work: A Cure for Capitalism*. Chicago: Haymarket Books.

Wolff, R.D. (2013) *Capitalism Hits the Fan: The Global Economic Meltdown and What to Do About It*, 2nd edition. Northampton: Interlink Publishing.

Wouk, H. (1952) *The Caine Mutiny*. London: Hodder & Stoughton.

Index